Number 150
Summer 2016

New Directions for Evaluation

Paul R. Brandon
Editor-in-Chief

Seven North American Evaluation Pioneers

David D. Williams
Editor

SEVEN NORTH AMERICAN EVALUATION PIONEERS
David D. Williams (ed.)
New Directions for Evaluation, no. 150
Paul R. Brandon, Editor-in-Chief

Microfilm copies of issues and articles are available in 16mm and 35mm, as well as microfiche in 105mm, through University Microfilms Inc., 300 North Zeeb Road, Ann Arbor, MI 48106-1346.

New Directions for Evaluation is indexed in Academic Search Alumni Edition (EBSCO Publishing), Education Research Complete (EBSCO Publishing), Higher Education Abstracts (Claremont Graduate University), SCOPUS (Elsevier), Social Services Abstracts (ProQuest), Sociological Abstracts (ProQuest), Worldwide Political Science Abstracts (ProQuest).

NEW DIRECTIONS FOR EVALUATION (ISSN 1097-6736, electronic ISSN 1534-875X) is part of The Jossey-Bass Education Series and is published quarterly by Wiley Subscription Services, Inc., A Wiley Company, at Jossey-Bass, One Montgomery Street, Suite 1200, San Francisco, CA 94104-4594.

SUBSCRIPTIONS for individuals cost $89 for U.S./Canada/Mexico/international. For institutions, $358 U.S.; $398 Canada/Mexico; $432 international. Electronic only: $89 for individuals all regions; $358 for institutions all regions. Print and electronic: $98 for individuals in the U.S., Canada, and Mexico; $122 for individuals for the rest of the world; $430 for institutions in the U.S.; $470 for institutions in Canada and Mexico; $504 for institutions for the rest of the world.

All issues are proposed by guest editors. For proposal submission guidelines, go to http://www.eval.org/p/cm/ld/fid=48. Editorial correspondence should be addressed to the Editor-in-Chief, Paul R. Brandon, University of Hawai'i at Mānoa, 1776 University Avenue, Castle Memorial Hall Rm 118, Honolulu, HI 96822-2463.

www.josseybass.com

Editorial Policy and Procedures

New Directions for Evaluation, a quarterly sourcebook, is an official publication of the American Evaluation Association. The journal publishes works on all aspects of evaluation, with an emphasis on presenting timely and thoughtful reflections on leading-edge issues of evaluation theory, practice, methods, the profession, and the organizational, cultural, and societal context within which evaluation occurs. Each issue of the journal is devoted to a single topic, with contributions solicited, organized, reviewed, and edited by one or more guest editors.

The editor-in-chief is seeking proposals for journal issues from around the globe about topics new to the journal (although topics discussed in the past can be revisited). A diversity of perspectives and creative bridges between evaluation and other disciplines, as well as chapters reporting original empirical research on evaluation, are encouraged. A wide range of topics and substantive domains are appropriate for publication, including evaluative endeavors other than program evaluation; however, the proposed topic must be of interest to a broad evaluation audience.

Journal issues may take any of several forms. Typically they are presented as a series of related chapters, but they might also be presented as a debate; an account, with critique and commentary, of an exemplary evaluation; a feature-length article followed by brief critical commentaries; or perhaps another form proposed by guest editors.

Submitted proposals must follow the format found via the Association's website at http://www.eval.org/Publications/NDE.asp. Proposals are sent to members of the journal's Editorial Advisory Board and to relevant substantive experts for single-blind peer review. The process may result in acceptance, a recommendation to revise and resubmit, or rejection. The journal does not consider or publish unsolicited single manuscripts.

Before submitting proposals, all parties are asked to contact the editor-in-chief, who is committed to working constructively with potential guest editors to help them develop acceptable proposals. For additional information about the journal, see the "Statement of the Editor-in-Chief" in the Spring 2013 issue (No. 137).

Paul R. Brandon, Editor-in-Chief
University of Hawai'i at Mānoa
College of Education
1776 University Avenue
Castle Memorial Hall, Rm. 118
Honolulu, HI 968222463
e-mail: nde@eval.org

CONTENTS

EDITOR'S NOTES[1]

The farther back you can look, the farther forward you are likely to see.
—Winston Churchill

valuation theorists (Fitzpatrick, 2013; Schwandt, 2003; Scriven, 1999; Stake, 2013) have suggested that evaluators should study how people evaluate both professionally and extraprofessionally (in daily life), to better understand these practices and build on them to encourage better practices. At the 2013 annual meeting of the American Evaluation Association (AEA2013), I chaired a symposium (Williams, 2013) in which Robert Stake, Marvin Alkin, Michael Scriven, Daniel Stufflebeam, Eleanor Chelimsky, Ernie House, and Michael Patton shared and interpreted stories from their extraprofessional as well as professional evaluation lives.

As they shared these memories and thoughts elicited during a series of interviews, I invited them to discuss possible connections between their stories and their professional evaluation theories and practices, which have been influential in the field of evaluation. During the interviews and through their AEA2013 presentations, they also explored how all these perspectives might affect the future of evaluation.

Although many other influential evaluators are participating in similar interviews documenting their memories of and reflections on their own evaluation lives (see a related AEA2014 session at Williams, 2014), this issue focuses on the stories and interpretations of the AEA2013 group. These individuals were some of the earliest and most influential evaluation participants who made themselves available when this project began. Some others passed away before I was able to involve them sufficiently. Those who participated were willing to tell their stories in enough detail to clarify their emerging values. The details enhance transferability by readers to other contexts, but because of length, only some stories are included in this issue. I am exploring multiple venues for sharing additional extraprofessional evaluation stories by these and other influential evaluators representing various ages, races, countries, and approaches.

These editor's notes introduce the need for better understanding the extraprofessional evaluation life experiences of evaluators. I also review the methods I used to sample, interview, and invite the evaluators to reflect on their experiences, share their reflections, and interpret their stories. After

[1]Thank you to six anonymous reviewers, Editor-in-Chief Paul Brandon, Sharon Black, Kathryn Ehlert, Thomas Ferrin, Susan Gong, and Jaquelyn Johnson for feedback on drafts of this manuscript.

listing several limitations, I introduce the rest of the issue, in which evaluators share their own accounts; a later-generation evaluator, Kushner, comments on the whole project; and I draw inferences about their values based
on their reflections.

Need

The field of evaluation, like social science generally, has been invited to
consider seriously related ideas from the humanities, philosophy, and many
practical fields. For example, Schwandt (2002) examined the field of evaluation practice and concluded that "when properly conceived as an activity
of teaching and learning resulting in an action-oriented self-understanding,
evaluation becomes more continuous with the ways we are as human beings
in our everyday lives" (p. xi). He claimed evaluators need to use

> a different kind of knowledge, variously spoken of as understanding or wise
> judgment [which] arises in a dialogue with others [and] refers to an ontology
> of relation—a way of understanding the self, a way we are as human beings
> in the world, or our ethical or moral orientation as human beings. (p. 6)

Schwandt noted further,

> A common ... assumption of ... evaluation is that the evaluator best serves
> society by aiming to redeem evaluation decision making from the parti-
> san, partial, allegedly often unreasonable and unreasoned world of everyday
> life ... by making it more rational [or] importing into everyday life some pro-
> cedure for evaluating human action that will not permit judgments of value
> to be tainted by personal preferences, mere tastes, old habits, or subjective
> wants and desires. (p. 13)

In response to his analysis of the situation, Schwandt suggested "we
explore evaluation as another way we are in the world, and bring our no-
tions of evaluating and evaluation practice closer to the realities of thinking
and doing in everyday life" (p. 17). Acting on this invitation has become a
major purpose of my research and of this issue.

Little is known about how people learn to evaluate and participate in
extraprofessional evaluative life experiences or how they relate those experiences to their participation in professional evaluations, either as evaluators or as stakeholders. Indeed, as Mark, Greene, and Shaw (2006, p. 2)
noted, "There is no consensus in the evaluation or the wider social science
communities about the relationship between the different kinds of knowledge that are entailed in more formal and more informal evaluative judgments." Therefore, as Schwandt (2003) suggested, we should study how
people evaluate in daily life, both to understand this dimension of being
human and to gain insight into and then improve evaluation practice.

Theorists and academicians have been proposing alternative ways to conceive of and conduct professional evaluation studies for over 50 years, and philosophers and other discipline leaders have discussed values and valuing as a human activity for thousands of years (Fitzpatrick, Sanders, & Worthen, 2003). However, very few studies have examined the lived experiences of evaluators, the subjects they evaluate, or the people for whom they conduct their evaluations (Baron, 2009). Similarly, the extraprofessional evaluations of everyday people are judged by most academicians as lacking sufficient rigor to be considered valuable in informing professional evaluations (Stufflebeam & Shinkfield, 2007), without documentation of how and why such everyday evaluations are conducted by stakeholders or by professional evaluators as part of their own extraprofessional lives.

A quick survey of human life reveals that evaluation happens in many different spheres. Educational movements encourage critical thinking by people of all ages, and some scholars consider the principles of critical thinking to be evaluation principles (Paul & Elder, 2007). Most scholarly disciplines teach novitiates the criteria and standards for successfully engaging in professional conversations. Performance disciplines in the arts, letters, and sciences identify and advocate standards for acceptability, and the field of evaluation, through a Joint Committee, has developed standards for judging the quality of evaluations of programs (Yarbrough, Shula, Hopson, & Caruthers, 2010), personnel (Gullickson & Howard, 2009), and student learning (Klinger et al., 2015), as well as guiding principles (American Evaluation Association, 2004) for evaluators in all disciplines.

In addition, families, churches, and other social groups teach their members values and standards of moral behavior, including what they consider to be appropriate intellectual and attitudinal performance. Observation as well as literature and popular culture make it obvious that all human beings use these values to conduct evaluations daily. But we know very little about how evaluators and other stakeholders develop their values, including their evaluative attitudes and skills; how they carry out the hundreds of evaluations they conduct daily; how they think and feel about this major dimension of human experience; or how these evaluations relate to professional evaluations in which people participate or which they are asked to consume.

Understanding the answers to these questions should be very important to the field of evaluation, as these answers could inform the critique and further development of evaluation theories and practices—which impact all of us, as we and our practices are constantly evaluated. Likewise, because evaluation is considered by some (e.g., Scriven, 1991) to be a *transdiscipline*, what is learned about evaluation practice and experience could impact all the disciplines it crosses and all the people who engage in evaluations, if they could be appropriately informed of principles to consider for improving their practices.

Since being introduced to the field of evaluation in 1974, I have studied, conducted, taught others, and been subjected to evaluations associated with most of the professional evaluation approaches written about beginning in the 1960s. In the 1990s, I acted on an increasing interest to know more about how people define and conduct evaluations in everyday life by asking interviewees the meaning they attached to *evaluation*. In the 2000s, I began to formalize this interest into studying (a) extraprofessional evaluation in daily life and (b) professional judgments that have not necessarily involved use of the principles from the professional field of evaluation (Hurteau & Williams, 2014), as well as professional evaluators' lives.

Focus

A developing literature (e.g., Gilovich, Griffin, & Kahneman, 2002; Kahneman, 2011; Klein, 2009) analyzes and critiques decision making as practiced by people generally as well as by decision makers professionally without necessarily involving those labeled as professional evaluators. In 2010, I began a formal study of everyday evaluation lives with people willing to sign my approved institutional review board consent form. I was hoping to follow Studs Terkel's (e.g., 1974) method of documenting a wide variety of self-reported experiences from people in all walks of life. I chose to focus on their ways of defining and actualizing their values and perceptions of evaluation through their daily choices. That interest and the nature of the associated case studies continue to guide me. In February 2012, I interviewed Bob Stake, who encouraged me to focus a part of my project on the evaluation lives of professional evaluators. Stake suggested some modifications to the research questions and gave me a list of people who might be willing to share their stories.

Subsequently, I have held case study conversations with scores of people and am contacting many more who conduct and/or write about professional evaluation. I anticipate these inquiries will continue for several years. I anticipate that the experiences and reflections of these individuals who have influenced the evaluation field will invite evaluators in all disciplines to address current and future challenges of both professional and extraprofessional evaluation creatively. I also want to capture these stories while these influential evaluators are still able and willing to share them.

I have assumed that understanding how influential theorists and practitioners think about their extraprofessional evaluation life experiences from childhood through adulthood and how they relate those experiences to their efforts to build evaluation theory and conduct professional evaluations could enlighten other evaluators as they make similar connections in their own lives. Similarly, readers who are working with stakeholders and evaluation project audiences might profitably make connections with their particular kinds of evaluations, and thus find ways to improve their practices.

Novelty and Timeliness

Nothing like this has been published, although inquiry related to these issues would appear to be useful to professional evaluators, theorists, and their stakeholders. In particular, influential creators of the field of evaluation have not described their extraprofessional evaluation experiences in life generally or related them to their theories and practices as professional evaluators. To address this need, I was searching for the values these influential people developed throughout their extraprofessional evaluation lives and ways they personally believe those values relate to their professional evaluations and theories.

Published documents that come closest to addressing the purpose of this issue are the oral history of evaluation articles in the *American Journal of Evaluation* (e.g., King, Shanker, Miller, & Mark, 2010; Miller, King, & Mark, 2008, 2009) on some of the most influential evaluators in the United States, two books by Alkin (2004, 2013), and a volume by Stufflebeam (2001). However, the focus of those publications is almost exclusively on the participants' professional evaluation lives, with relatively little exploration of how they think their life experiences with extraprofessional evaluation might connect to their professional evaluation work.

To address these gaps in the literature, I invited professional evaluators to explore their answers to these questions:

1. What have you brought to and built into your influential evaluation practice and theory from your general evaluation life?
2. What implications do you find in your own experience that might benefit the field of professional evaluation?

Methods

In 2010, I began conducting case studies (Stake, 1995, 2006, 2010) through conversational interviews (Seidman, 2006) with a wide variety of people in various professions other than professional evaluation. In early 2012, I began contacting several influential professional evaluators and theorists who might be willing to participate and soon had interviews with Alkin, Scriven, and Stufflebeam. Later Chelimsky, House, and Patton responded to my invitations, and interviews followed.

Through an emerging purposive sampling process, I continue contacting professional evaluators and inviting them to participate, hoping to expand the number and variety of cases to be shared. Generalization in the sense of statistical probability is not the goal of this work, even anticipating many more interviews with influential evaluators. Rather, the objectives of this qualitative inquiry include discovery of the particular and often unique experiences of participants, as well as some possible themes across interviewees, with detailed accounts of their experiences and views. Thick descriptions of the participants' experiences should enhance readers' ability to transfer the lessons learned from these cases to their own lives, practices, and theories according to personal judgment.

Follow-up interviews invited individuals to elaborate on their stories and on patterns they and I had identified during previous interviews through review of audio recordings, field notes, presentations at AEA, and draft reports. I collaborated with each interviewee and with research assistants to identify relevant stories, interpretive participant comments, and cross-case themes and patterns, while acknowledging that these are self-reports of participants' past experiences, including interpretations through their personal perspectives (limited by associated subjective memory).

The interpretations of the case study data are based on analysis procedures following Stake's (2006, 2010) and Spradley's (1979) recommendations. Through interview questions, I facilitated each individual's retelling of life experiences, inviting the participants to comment in the context of the stories in their own articles of this issue.

The final article includes comments by all participants on the articles of their colleagues and on my interpretations. My interpretive comments were clarified by three principal strategies:

1. Identifying key ideas associated with the interviewees' values, including how they acquired and used those values and how their use of values has bridged their extraprofessional and professional evaluation lives.
2. Looking for similarities and differences in key ideas across cases.
3. Selecting statements to quote to illustrate the themes and suggest possible implications of theme interpretations for the future of evaluation.

The case studies were conducted with careful attention to the following criteria of trustworthiness recommended by Lincoln and Guba (1985):

1. *Triangulation,* using multiple cases and interviews
2. *Negative case analysis,* searching for and exploring inconsistencies within stories told by each interviewee and across cases
3. *Member checking,* asking the evaluators who have told their own stories to check my interpretations
4. *Peer review,* having each article examined by Kushner and by each of the other interviewees
5. *Thick description,* using interviewees' own words and including explanations of the meanings they attached to their stories
6. *Audit trail,* preparing a carefully documented audit trail and making it available upon request

All participants gave informed consent, agreeing to tell their own stories without anonymity.

Limitations

I thank reviewers of early drafts of this issue for noting potential limitations, including sampling, reflection, causation, emerging framework, and novelty.

Sampling

Only seven evaluators are included in this issue, six of them males. If these case studies were intended to reveal generalizable causal links between extraprofessional and professional evaluations, this sampling strategy would be inappropriate. However, interviewees were selected because they represent an important subset of the originators of the evaluation profession. The sampling limitation is still relevant and is being addressed by other publications based on more of the stories told by these seven, along with stories from many more evaluators around the world, including all eras since the 1950s, representing diverse groups of men and women from multiracial, multiethnic, multiaged subsets of professional evaluators. Still the results represented in this issue are limited to the seven people included and the particular stories selected from those they volunteered.

Reflection

Because these evaluators have contributed few or no publications recording their extraprofessional evaluation experiences and because this study began after several of them had retired from active professional evaluation practice, data collection has been limited to interviews inviting the evaluators to reflect on and share their life experiences and to make connections among those experiences when I asked them to do so. Obviously, the results are personal recollections in response to an inquirer. Thus, we can assume they are subjective, personal, and biased in unknowable ways. The alternative would be not to request or report on the stories of these distinguished individuals, which seemed a greater limitation than the risk of subjectivity.

Causality

Although causal relationships may be hypothesized based on the particular stories collected in these case studies, identifying and testing such hypotheses was not the purpose of this research; readers seeking causal explanations may consider this a limitation. But I approached this inquiry from a paradigm of understanding rather than explanation. I sought narrative accounts in which the evaluators interviewed might describe their life experiences, think about them aloud, and speculate on how these experiences might relate to their professional evaluation experiences and to the future of the field of evaluation they helped create, without being required to test those connections for causality. Future research might address this limitation.

Emerging Framework

When I began this work, some critics asked me to explain my theoretical framework for gathering and interpreting the case data. I replied that I was inviting interviewees to define the questions, answers, and dimensions around which their own experiences might be interpreted most authentically in terms of the meanings they associated with them. Therefore, the two research questions listed earlier guided the interviews and interpretations very loosely, with many invitations to the evaluators to redirect them according to their emerging frameworks for meaning. This is also the reason they all eventually wrote their own interpretive articles, in response to drafts of their articles based on their interview statements and their AEA2013 presentations. Out of this member-checking and interviewee-driven process, I identified multiple themes in each case and many across the cases. However, because of the focus on the particular experiences of these seven and due to limited space, this issue focuses on telling their stories and only briefly addressing the most prominent theme that crossed all cases regarding their values.

Novelty

The seven authors are so well published that my space is inadequate to review their work. Thus, it may seem that they or others have written so much about their evaluation approaches and experiences that there is little new to understand. However, because the focus of this research is on the extraprofessional evaluation life experiences of these evaluators, their articles share stories unknown to most readers and for the first time explore some of the meaning they associate with those experiences. The authors' views are tied to their professional evaluation theories, approaches, and experiences, which have been published widely. So though they may seem familiar to avid readers of these authors, the novelty is in the connections the authors make between their well-known professional evaluation ideas and stories and their untold extraprofessional examples.

Preview

The evaluators were interviewed, and their articles are presented in this sequence: Stake, Alkin, Scriven, Stufflebeam, Chelimsky, House, and Patton. They wrote their articles with my collaboration, by participating in interviews and thinking about stories and issues raised; drafting their own articles to reflect their thoughts; reviewing, revising, and approving my rendition of their articles; and reviewing interpretations made in the final article by all authors. Then, in the penultimate article, another seasoned evaluator, Kushner, offers his thoughts about the accounts and interpretations offered throughout the issue, commenting on what he surmises to be some implications for the future of evaluation.

In the final article, I share a prominent theme and subthemes I found while studying all seven cases, concluding that these evaluators' extraprofessional evaluation lives are filled with experiences that formed and tested their adherence to particular values. They have struggled to understand, modify, and implement these values through their definitions, explanations, and applications to professional evaluations and theories. Also in the final article, the seven evaluators comment briefly on one another's articles and possible implications for the future of evaluation theory and practice.

The issue ends by inviting readers to think about possible implications for their own and their stakeholders' evaluation lives. The entire document invites readers to relate to evaluation, not as a technology, but as a values-based activity involving their values and those of other participants in their evaluations.

References

Alkin, M. (2004). *Evaluation roots* (1st ed.). Thousand Oaks, CA: Sage.

Alkin, M. (2013). *Evaluation roots* (2nd ed.). Thousand Oaks, CA: Sage.

American Evaluation Association. (2004). *Guiding principles for evaluators.* Retrieved from http://www.eval.org/p/cm/ld/fid=51.

Baron, M. E. (2009). *Understanding how evaluators deal with multiple stakeholders.* (Unpublished doctoral dissertation), Brigham Young University, Provo, UT. Retrieved from http://contentdm.lib.byu.edu/cdm4/item_viewer.php?CISOROOT=/ETD&CISOPTR=1956&CISOBOX=1&REC=1

Fitzpatrick, J. L., Sanders, J. R., & Worthen, B. R. (2003). *Program evaluation: Alternative approaches and practical guidelines* (3rd ed.). Boston, MA: Allyn and Bacon.

Fitzpatrick, J. (2013). Call for AEA presentations and announcement of theme in Evaluation 2013 Presidential Strand Theme, Evaluation Practice in the Early 21st Century. Retrieved from http://www.eval.org/p/cm/ld/fid=166

Gilovich, T., Griffin, D. W., & Kahneman, D. (Eds.). (2002). *Heuristics and biases: The psychology of intuitive judgment.* New York, NY: Cambridge University Press.

Gullickson, A. R., & Howard, B. B. (2009). *The personnel evaluation standards: How to assess systems for evaluating educators* (2nd ed.). Thousand Oaks, CA: Corwin Press.

Hurteau, M., & Williams, D. D. (2014). Credible judgment: Combining truth, beauty and justice. In J. C. Griffith & B. Montrosse-Moorhead (Eds.), *Revisiting truth, beauty, and justice: Evaluating with validity in the 21st century. New Directions for Evaluation, 142,* 45–56.

Kahneman, D. (2011). *Thinking, fast and slow.* New York, NY: Farrar, Straus, & Giroux.

King, J. A., Shanker, V., Miller, R. L., & Mark, M. M. (2010). The oral history of evaluation: The professional development of Marvin C. Alkin. *American Journal of Evaluation, 31*(2), 266–277.

Klein, G. (2009). *Streetlights and shadows: Searching for the keys to adaptive decision making.* Cambridge, MA: MIT Press.

Klinger, D. A., McDivitt, P. R., Howard, B. B., Munoz, M. A., Rogers, W. T., & Wylie, E. C. (2015). *The classroom assessment standards for PreK–12 teachers.* Kindle Direct Press.

Lincoln, Y. S., & Guba, E. G. (1985). *Naturalistic inquiry.* Newbury Park, CA: Sage.

Mark, M. M., Greene, J. C., & Shaw, I. F. (2006). Introduction: The evaluation of policies, programs, and practices. In M. M. Mark, J. C. Greene, & I. F. Shaw (Eds.), *The Sage handbook of evaluation* (pp. 1–30). Thousand Oaks, CA: Sage.

Miller, R. L., King, J. A., & Mark, M. M. (2008). The oral history of evaluation: The professional development of Daniel L. Stufflebeam. *American Journal of Evaluation*, 29(4), 555–571.

Miller, R. L., King, J. A., & Mark, M. M. (2009). The oral history of evaluation: The professional development of Eleanor Chelimsky. *American Journal of Evaluation*, 30(2), 232–244.

Paul, R., & Elder, L. (2007). *The miniature guide to critical thinking concepts and tools*. Dillon Beach, CA: Foundation for Critical Thinking Press. Retrieved from http://www.duluth.umn.edu/~jetterso/documents/CriticalThinking.pdf

Schwandt, T. A. (2002). *Evaluation practice reconsidered*. New York, NY: Peter Lang.

Schwandt, T. A. (2003, July). Back to the rough ground! Beyond theory to practice in evaluation. *Evaluation, 9*, 353–364.

Scriven, M. (1991). *Evaluation thesaurus* (4th ed.). Newbury Park, CA: Sage.

Scriven, M. (1999). Presidential address. Presented at the Annual Conference of the American Evaluation Association, Orlando, FL.

Seidman, I. (2006). *Interviewing as qualitative research: A guide for researchers in education and the social sciences* (3rd ed.). New York, NY: Teachers College Press.

Spradley, J. P. (1979). *The ethnographic interview*. Belmont, CA: Wadsworth.

Stake, R. E. (1995). *The art of case study research*. Thousand Oaks, CA: Sage.

Stake, R. E. (2006). *Multiple case study analysis*. New York, NY: Guilford Press.

Stake, R. E. (2010). *Qualitative research: Studying how things work*. New York, NY: Guilford Press.

Stake, R. E. (2013). The people and the profession. In Stewart Donaldson (Ed.), *The future of evaluation in society, a tribute to Michael Scriven* (pp. 109–117). Charlotte, NC: Information Age Publishing.

Stufflebeam, D. L. (2001). Evaluation models. *New Directions for Evaluation, 89*, 7–98.

Stufflebeam, D. L., & Shinkfield, A. J. (2007). *Evaluation theory, models, and applications*. San Francisco, CA: Jossey-Bass.

Terkel, S. (1974). *Working: People talk about what they do all day and how they feel about what they do*. New York, NY: Pantheon/Random House.

Williams, D. D. (2013, October). Themes from Case Studies of Evaluators' Lives. Symposium organized and presented with Marv Alkin, Eleanor Chelimsky, Michael Patton, Robert Stake, Ernie House, Michael Scriven, and Daniel Stufflebeam at the Annual American Evaluation Association meetings, Washington, DC. Retrieved from http://comm.eval.org/communities/resources/viewdocument/?DocumentKey=7b1fd99f-53a1–45af-8557–261c038a5a04

Williams, D. D. (2014, October). Case Studies of Evaluators' Lives. Symposium organized and presented with Marv Alkin, Rodney Hopson, Gene Glass, Jody Fitzpatrick, Hallie Preskill, Jane Davidson, Stewart Donaldson, Paul Brandon at the Annual American Evaluation Association meetings, Denver, CO. Retrieved from http://comm.eval.org/viewdocument/?DocumentKey=7c326f4b-34ae-43a3–8098-f49fd410c939

Yarbrough, D. B., Shula, L. M., Hopson, R. K., & Caruthers, F. A. (2010). *The program evaluation standards: A guide for evaluators and evaluation users* (3rd ed.). Thousand Oaks, CA: Corwin Press.

David Dwayne Williams

DAVID D. WILLIAMS is a professor of Instructional Psychology and Technology at Brigham Young University.

Stake, R. (2016). Are my professional evaluation dispositions to be found in my early life experiences? In D. D. Williams (Ed.), *Seven North American evaluation pioneers. New Directions for Evaluation, 150,* 17–24.

1

Are My Professional Evaluation Dispositions to Be Found in My Early Life Experiences?

Robert E. Stake

Abstract

Having searched for prescient stories from his early life, Robert Stake passes on these observations from recollections, interviews with David Williams, and symposium sessions of the American Evaluation Association in 2012 and 2013. He speaks of opposing views of evaluation held by his parents, perhaps eventually appearing in his writings. He reflects on ordinary evaluation decisions he made about getting married, going to graduate school, and raising children. He does not see such early experiences much paralleling or informing his professional evaluation theories and practices. Readers may see values he found extraprofessionally marking his professional work. © 2016 Wiley Periodicals, Inc., and the American Evaluation Association.

Experiences in Evaluation

When, with David's questioning, I probed my memory to find early experiences that might have helped shape my work as a professional evaluator, I became persuaded that they all did, but that none did. I found no particular precedents, no epiphanies, no critical incidents, no deliberations that steered my way into the field. I did find consistencies with the kind of evaluator I have become. To provide a filter for what is to follow, I will indicate what kind of evaluator I think I have become.

NEW DIRECTIONS FOR EVALUATION, no. 150, Summer 2016 © 2016 Wiley Periodicals, Inc., and the American Evaluation Association. Published online in Wiley Online Library (wileyonlinelibrary.com) • DOI: 10.1002/ev.20185

1. I believe you need to get close to the action.
2. I believe that immediate and situated issues are better conceptual structures for designing evaluation than goals or general standards.
3. I believe that a single criterion or indicator variable is usually simplistic and sometimes leads to damaging side effects.
4. I believe that local and overarching contexts shape meanings and outcomes and need to be accounted for in a comprehensive evaluation.
5. I rely heavily on intuitive understanding of merit.

But this perhaps is taking too much out of David's hands. He's the one distilling the accounts and comparing experiences across evaluators to report how ordinary growing up may create propensities for becoming a professional evaluator.

Portents?

I grew up in a rural village (no more than a few miles from Ralph Tyler's hometown), with a father who, although long a member of the Village Board (but perhaps because of it), saw government as inefficient and insensitive, sometimes mean. Had he had the chance, he probably would have supported moratoria on government. My mother was active in the Nebraska Republican party but, unlike her cabal, was enchanted by Eleanor Roosevelt, early and late.

My father was a pharmacist, proud of his care in mixing chemistries to make medicine. With depression-day doctors filling their own prescriptions, we survived by selling ice cream and sundries. It didn't make much difference whether "jerking" sodas or selling wallpaper to get through hard times—it was done with care, using "quality" stuff to make a good product. Dad made sure of the ingredients, that the chocolate had aged and that the carbonated water was 40°F or cooler. So ideas of caretaking materials and wiping the spill were prominent—with me unaware I was getting advice for life's work.

My mother was a teacher. She was inclined to say, "You should grade children's work in terms of the effect that it will have on them more than in terms of whether they deserved an A or a C or an F." There was a difference in mother's and father's behaviorist leanings. His were that you should be sensitive to who deserved a reward. And she said you should carefully look at the potential effect of the rewards. The two views did not converge; they remained epistemologies undiscussed.

I cared perhaps too much about my own grades and my standing in the eyes of elders, certainly teachers, certainly the widows across the street, but I do not think it a philosophy for an evaluation career. It seemed that formal evaluation came about me, suddenly lighted, suddenly present. Somebody needed something called "an evaluation." I had some available time. I had no sense of evaluation as a calling, a talent or skill, but maybe sometimes a service—a need for doing it. It might be art or technology.

I often thought of evaluation as competitive enterprise, in the way mother's roses were judged at the flower show down at the church. Or students in a music contest, judged by a music teacher. (If my 5-years-younger brother competed, it was on an orthogonal track.) When my four children heard "The unexamined life is not worth living," they quickly added, "but neither is the over-..." Competition was everywhere. Without giving up my winnings, I became opposed to competition in school. Now I urge that comparison be downplayed in program evaluation settings.

I joined the Navy, selected a graduate school, raised a family. I've made many personal decisions. I probably have avoided a larger number. Delaying sometimes opens options. I may list pros and cons—more for the purpose of being inclusive, less to weigh the matter. I don't recall thinking of pharmaceutical scales as symbolizing the choice of action. I don't follow the common rules of deliberation. I'm inclined to contemplate the options one by one, more than one against the others, feeling experience and intuition will tell me the better choice. Perhaps this lets my emotions interfere. I don't know.

Many times the choice to stand pat was more comfortable than the choice to move on. Of course, I thought of alternatives, but in retrospect it regularly seemed I resisted the flow. Did I trust too little the delineation of pros and cons? Intuition will take into account factors I haven't yet seen. Is it not better to become personally familiar with the headings than logically precise with the ingredients? I guess I am my mother's boy.

Criticism

Reflecting further on personality, I find myself straddling the fence on criticism, even though I write advocating it. My mother had trouble seeing ill in people, save William Jennings Bryan, Adolf Hitler, and the boy who choked me unconscious at school. (I had my stint as bullied.) My father deplored quite a few more. I deplore the overpromisers, so joined with Michael Scriven in taking goal statements lightly.

I am not an inveterate doubter. I don't quickly say "But why?" I'm likely to say "Okay, that's the way it is." It takes a person who is rational and skeptical, a person protecting community and system, to say "Let's evaluate with precision."

Through 87 years I have had a voluminous safety net. Sometimes, even though I've made decisions poorly, I find the new track comfortable or the old welcoming me back. Ice cream alone didn't buy that much safety net. Some evaluators I admire most are those who save their criticisms for the most adept.

Graduate School

One way to understand my evaluation life is to look at the critical decisions I made, like avoiding Greek fraternities, marrying, and choosing a graduate school. Richard Madden, a cousin of mine, was Dean of Education at San Diego State. We lived nearby. A number of school districts around the country called him in for consultation. He authored elementary textbooks and relied heavily on standardized student achievement testing to bolster his advice. In 1954, the profession of evaluation had not arrived. I admired his ability to connect district-level curricular decisions to test performance. But Richard suggested I go elsewhere for graduate work. It might be he knew he was on thin ice. He suggested Illinois, and I applied, then reconsidered and returned to Nebraska. Richard said he was doing interpretative measurement, not the comprehensive field study that I now promote as "program evaluation."

For doctoral study, it was an easy choice. I applied to Princeton and Minnesota. Princeton replied first and offered me fellowship money beyond dreaming, $11,000 per year, as I recall. I was thinking, "I've had better accept before it goes away." Minnesota responded a few weeks later, but I had already made the decision. Had I been more rational, I would have investigated and found out that Minnesota had an educational orientation, which I preferred, while Princeton did not.

So I went to Princeton in psychology and was assigned education chores that no one else in the department wanted. They had many faculty members teaching, counseling, grading maybe without knowing as much education as I did, which wasn't much. And in so doing, I advanced what became a lifelong commitment to education, as my mother had, mixing it with testing, as Richard had.

In 1963, after I'd been 5 years at the University of Nebraska, Tom Hastings persuaded me to become his assistant directing the Illinois Statewide Testing Program. By the end of the decade I was seeing the birth of a cult: the cult of educational accountability, the cult of performance objectives. Its co-Messiahs were Robert Kennedy and Robert Macnamara. President Johnson had declared war on two fronts: Vietnam and poverty. He needed outcomes to be counted. Psychometrics delivered. And soon came Sputnik.

It was an impressive defense force. At Illinois were Hastings, Lee Cronbach, Jack Easley, Mike Atkin, many others. A little further away were Michael Scriven, Bob Ingle, Don Campbell, Bill Gephart. And soon to arrive were Ernie House, Gene Glass, Gordon Hoke, and Terry Elofson. We made plans to resist the cult. The counterforce to Russian technology and management by objectives turned out to be program evaluation. I didn't catch on quickly to what they meant. Tom and Lee were writing a proposal to create CIRCE, the Center for Instructional Research and Curriculum Evaluation. I tried to help, but I didn't know what to say. I didn't understand

NEW DIRECTIONS FOR EVALUATION • DOI: 10.1002/ev

what we might soon be doing that we in instructional research and psychometrics weren't already doing: measuring and comparing. I didn't operationalize "educational quality" well. I didn't see what my mother saw in Eleanor Roosevelt.

In a while I got the idea from Jack Easley that we needed to pay close attention to what was going on in the classroom. From Tom Hastings I got the idea that we needed to pay as much attention to contexts as to test scores. At that time there was the Social Science Education Consortium, a network of studies sponsored by the National Science Foundation to develop precollege curricula. At their meetings, Cronbach, Ron Lippitt, Irving Morrissett, and Scriven were talking about curriculum project evaluation, strange (to me) things about user needs and meta-evaluation.

In time we formed an Evaluation Network, a May 12 Group, an Evaluation Research Society. Those were good old days, groping along. Dan Stufflebeam, Marv Alkin, Eva Baker, Egon Guba, Wayne Welch. For all their charm, Ralph Tyler and Jim Popham left me agitated by their concept of objectives.

For me, 1966 was the beginning of the turning point. Cronbach had written that evaluators were not paying enough attention to curriculum developers' needs. Teachers weren't understanding how they were supposed to change their teaching; it wasn't enough to give them better teacher workbooks and guidelines to assign homework. But what? Did they need mentoring or workshop experiences, teacher centers and communities of practice? Cronbach argued that evaluators needed to be part of a system to help teachers work things out—a kind of formative evaluation.

Scriven responded, saying more or less, "Wait a minute, that's not unimportant, but evaluation shouldn't be defined as service. Evaluation has to seek out the good lessons, the good credentials, the good supplementary materials. Teaching materials are not good simply because they are acceptable to teachers, but because they are built on sound conceptualizations. Given a program, evaluators have to figure out what is meritorious about its teaching and learning."

I remember their personalities. Cronbach didn't want to argue. He didn't say "Let's look at quality broadly." He said, "Let's do this because here's where the projects are hurting." Each had different advice. Michael would point out the flaws in Lee's position, and Lee would pay little attention to Michael's. So in 1966 Tom Hastings and I arranged to have it argued out. We invited a dozen or so people to the Illini Union for a day. I was still listening mostly to Tom and Ben Bloom and other testing friends, believing we could make our tests bear the load for program evaluation. (Even 4 years later, Bloom continued to declare that psychometric testing should be the heart of educational evaluation.) But after this one day, I thought, "Testing is not going to do it. We are going to have to arrange something bigger." In the days to follow, I wrote my paper on the "countenance" of evaluation (Stake, 1967). I remember one critical moment. As we got out of the car, Lee said,

"We need a social anthropologist." It took me years to grasp it. So perhaps 1966 was when I began to become what I am today.

Case Studies

By 1967, I had an inkling that we might need naturalistic case studies—their experientiality, dialogues, and contexts. At East Anglia, Barry MacDonald had been hired by Lawrence Stenhouse to evaluate the Humanities Curriculum Project (HCP). Lawrence told Barry he could not tell him how to evaluate, but he was to find out what was happening when kids argued social problems after reading the controversial HCP materials. When Barry visited Illinois, he showed us how he and David Hamilton and David Jenkins expected to use case studies.

In 1971, Barry started the "Cambridge Conferences," partly to intensify talk about case studies. I was not persuaded of case study centrality until much later. But soon I could see what McDonald was doing with his SAFARI study: closely observing campus use of computers to support instruction and writing case studies exposing academic and bureaucratic narrowness. I thought that made sense. But it had too much political advocacy for me. They were writing case studies showing that in this national promotion of instructional computers the orientation of government and industry was far from democratic. I didn't like being so political, but I did see they were revealing new complexities of university instruction.

Statewide Testing

One of the biggest decisions at CIRCE was the decision to end the Illinois Statewide Testing Program. We had provided school counselors in over 400 Illinois schools with scores on academic aptitudes and reasoning abilities. It had supported our research, as well as giving opportunities to hire several graduate students and to gather with distant colleagues to discuss testing practicalities. But our tests needed expensive revision, larger schools were creating their own testing programs, and scores were increasingly being used as indicators of school accountability. We decided to opt out and concentrate on program evaluation. How did we make this decision? After months of talking, termination just grew on us. We were assured the University of Illinois would let us use our good spaces for the new purpose. But if I had been more cautious or used better reasoning, I might have anticipated that the campus support for personnel and spaces would diminish, maybe end. In time we could do little evaluation research without external funding.

We were operating under the idea that many people, professional and lay, would like to know what we were learning about educational values, about different perceptions of goodness in particular evaluands. Gradually we realized that few cared or that times had changed. I remember Ernie House coming back to CIRCE from a meeting at the State Office of Public

Instruction quoting an associate superintendent saying, "Don't give us all these conditionals: 'If this would happen and that would happen, you can expect these to happen.'" He continued, "We don't want such complexity. You tell us what's good and we'll figure out how we can use it to support what we're already going to do."

I saw these dismissive remarks about evaluation first as irresponsible but later as inevitable. In program evaluation, I thought, we are dealing not with the whole truth but with a piece of it. I was reluctant to give up the foundational role for research. I wanted to preserve the belief that quality of teaching and learning can be found in a weighted sum of attributes.

But eventually I could not justify the weighted sum. We should not be claiming "This is the way it is!" We think we can say, "This is better than nothing," but even that is unwarranted. The total of attributes we have summed is sometimes worse than no formal data at all. The meagre indicator oversimplifies. It misrepresents. It reduces caution. So I don't promote weighted sums and comparisons any more. I prefer holistic observation, a little measurement, and opportunities to talk it over. It's insufficient, but easier to recognize as avoiding the facade of truth. (I recognize that anyone may hypothesize the experience of quality to an aggregate of judged criteria.)

Countenance

I wrote the countenance paper to answer the question of what data are eligible for consideration. What is relevant for careful collection of judgments and reflection? You try to avoid simple judgments. You work at making situated judgments, just as you make multiple measurements and descriptions. At the end of that paper I added a few comparative allusions, possible steps towards the conduct of evaluation. But they had no practical consequence. The paper was still about, "What could people be using to evaluate?" I didn't invent anything. With 13 boxes for data: antecedents, transactions and outcomes, *et cetera*, I categorized. Many evaluators were using too few categories to make evaluation comprehensive.

A few called it "the countenance model." It wasn't a model any more than the periodic table or a cheese shop. It was just a menu. I still needed to write about how to find merit and worth and significance. I needed to write something about methods as Dan Stufflebeam, Scriven, and Peter Rossi just had. Then came to my mind Jack Easley's ideas about personal inquiry into situation, problem, and dialogue. I saw Jack's ideas as—yes—responsive. I was working on art education projects with Elliot Eisner, Lou Smith, and Kathryn Bloom, and felt the need for an evaluation style comfortable to them as well as to science people. My evaluations had to be rooted in what was happening at the school. By "Responsive 1973" (Stake, 1973), I was saying far more than I did in "Countenance 1967"—that you need to seek quality, diverse observations, ample redundancy and deliberative judgments.

NEW DIRECTIONS FOR EVALUATION • DOI: 10.1002/ev

Standards

In the eighties, I thought we needed to find better statements of standards. But I abandoned that hope. Certainly they are not in Common Core. Such political standards are phantasmagoria—without substance, without depth. Ask committees their standards and you get aspirations. Organize teaching around standards and you diminish experiential learning. Instead, I looked for something tangible, behavioral, unique to the evaluand, and contextual to fixate on quality. One morning, getting out of bed, the word *responsive* popped again in my head. I knew immediately it was what I wanted to call my approach: responsive evaluation. Gradually, social anthropology had become clear.

I have turned this paper into what I ended with, not what I started with. Sorry, David. My snippets haven't made good links between early life and the field of evaluation. At the outset above I characterized my evaluation foci on experiential engagement, issue conceptualization, multiple criteria, contextual constraint, and intuitive judgment. There is no precision of ingredients. There is little conditioning of learners. Is what we have more Zeitgeist than great men? Let's not compare.

I don't require an objective reality. I told my mother as we boarded the train, "You sit on that side and I on this, so we don't miss a thing."

References

Stake, R. E. (1967). The countenance of educational evaluation. *Teachers College Record*, *68*, 523–540.

Stake, R. E. (1973). Program evaluation, particularly responsive evaluation. In K. Härnqvist, U. Lundgren, & E. Wallin (Eds.), *New trends in evaluation, No. 35* (pp. 1–20). Göteborg, Sweden: Institute of Education, University of Göteborg.

ROBERT E. STAKE *is the director of the CIRCE Evaluation Center and is an emeritus professor of education at the University of Illinois, Urbana-Champaign.*

Alkin, M. (2016). Bunts, bloop singles, sacrifices, hard base running, and lots of luck. In
D. D. Williams (Ed.), *Seven North American evaluation pioneers. New Directions for Evaluation, 150*, 25–32.

2

Bunts, Bloop Singles, Sacrifices, Hard Base Running, and Lots of Luck

Marvin Alkin

Abstract

Alkin shares stories about his own evaluation life that he prepared for the American Evaluation Association (AEA) 2013 symposium session, based on his responses in interviews conducted by David Williams and on his earlier writings. He briefly mentions his father's influence on his values and extraprofessional evaluations before giving several examples of evaluation experiences he had as a teacher and counselor, as a university student, as a new faculty member, and as a home buyer—all before or while learning about the field of evaluation. He explores how an accumulation of experiences throughout his career and life provided opportunities for him to apply what he learned in his extraprofessional evaluation life to the formal approaches he took in conducting and writing about professional evaluation. © 2016 Wiley Periodicals, Inc., and the American Evaluation Association.

Experiences in Evaluation

I have no home run stories to tell. I feel very much like the baseball batter who comes to the plate after Babe Ruth hits a World Series grand slam homer. To my knowledge, I have no single momentous event that shaped me as a person and subsequently as an evaluator. My stories and other shaping events are a series of bunts, bloop singles, hard base running, et cetera—the same combination (along with good pitching) that the UCLA baseball team used to sweep all postseason games and win the 2013 College World Series.

A Bunt

My father was a grocer. He had a small market, and we lived a comfortable middle class life with no strife. Indeed, the only conflict (if you want to call it that) was that, in my mind, he made assertions without sufficient evidence to back them up. I would say, "How do you know?" He was also too nice, too kind, and too nonjudgmental. He saw good in everyone. Even when people took advantage of him, he would say, "He meant well." I was a bratty kid who was bothered by his acquiescence and continually argued with him and demanded to know how he could say that—"What's the evidence?" and again, "How do you know that?" You might say that this search for rational knowledge was the beginning of my evaluation career. My father died at age 59, and I have felt guilty ever since about my "over the top" rational behavior. Maybe there are times to respect instinct and experience.

A Bloop Single

I suppose that I have always had an orientation toward data and numbers. Thus, I actually was led to majoring in mathematics in college. After completing my degree in mathematics, I obtained a teaching credential and taught mathematics at the high school level. I loved teaching. I love teaching to this day. Communication of ideas appeals to me. But even more so, I enjoy attempting to "read" students and to determine whether real communication is taking place. Seeking to comprehend where they are coming from and whether they understand the material has been a part of the way that I view teaching. I suppose this translates as an evaluator into trying to picture stakeholders (potential users) and understand them—to perceive their point of view and the total context.

Further, an important part of my teaching then, as now, involves creating situations in which people can learn by doing—by role-playing. When teaching the lowest-level general mathematics class in high school, I created elaborate schemes to budget picnics and other events. Today I use scenarios and role-playing as an active part of every class I teach. In my Evaluation Procedures class, I establish simulated contexts, and my students and I role-play evaluators and primary users. In my Evaluation Theory class, students role-play major theorists (some of you who are reading this) in a confrontational game show format similar to "Meeting of the Minds," an early Steve Allen PBS program (see Alkin & Christie, 2002). Devising simulations and playing roles are important parts of the way that I do evaluation. I present scenarios to test whether the primary users' questions really get at what is considered important. Scenarios and role-playing are also a part of the a priori valuing procedure that I use with primary stakeholders.

NEW DIRECTIONS FOR EVALUATION • DOI: 10.1002/ev

A Walk

While teaching, I took a master's degree in counseling and guidance and afterward had several years of experience as a high school counselor. Dealing with students' personal problems and helping them to understand and work toward their goals sensitized me to dealing with others in nonthreatening, understanding ways, and further added to my future evaluation repertoire. As an evaluator, I am very attentive to the evaluator's need to use a variety of social skills that put stakeholders at ease while patiently and forcefully reaching a reasonable conclusion. This has strengthened the way that I work with users in framing an evaluation.

Hard Base Running and a Lucky Bounce

I thought my career path was in school administration and that I might start out as a school principal. Thus, while working in the school district, I started progress toward obtaining a school administrative credential. As a first step, I took a class in school case law at Stanford University. I missed one of the first classes because it coincided with my son's birth, and I went to the professor the following week before class asking for the assignment so that I might make it up. He referred me to his graduate assistant. Class time came that day, and the professor proceeded to ask students for an analysis of the first of the law cases assigned for that week. Turning to his roll book and examining the first name on the list, he called on me (a "benefit" of having a name that begins with "A"). I explained that I had not read any of the cases and could not answer. He persisted in urging me to try, which of course was impossible. He continued for what seemed like an interminable amount of time.

I was totally embarrassed and angry. I proceeded over the next 10 weeks to know just about everything about every case in the textbook and many of its precedents. After I responded correctly to every hypothetical situation he presented to the class, he subsequently refused to call on me. I also spent endless hours in the law school library preparing the legal brief that was the final assignment and turned it in. The final exam came and we brought our exams to the professor's office. Professor H. Thomas James looked at me and asked, "Are you a student in the Law School?"

"No."

"Are you a PhD student in political science?"

"No."

"Are you in our doctoral program?"

"No."

He handed me a 3 × 5 card, asked me to fill it out, and said, "When you are ready to get a doctorate, let me know and I will see that you are taken care of financially."

I don't want to ever be put in a position where I am embarrassed. Therefore, I work hard, am meticulous in my preparation, and have never been late on an evaluation report or an evaluation writing commitment. I'm usually early. Timeliness and attention to detail are part of my evaluation DNA.

A Bunt

My graduate experience at Stanford in working toward the doctorate in school administration was beneficial. It got me into thinking about administrators and their information needs. How could I, as a school administrator, better improve my program? What would be the sources of data that would help to inform my decisions? Further, the particular emphasis of my studies (economics/finance) squarely placed me into thinking about cost-benefit and cost-effectiveness analyses. These experiences certainly helped to shape (and were thus part of) my evaluation career.

A Bloop Single

During my doctoral studies, I had an interesting experience related to the doctoral qualifying examination. Stanford at that time required all students to answer an exam question in social foundations and one in psychological foundations, along with a question in their major field. Professor Larry Thomas, an educational philosopher, supervised the social foundations question. He had a standing invitation to students to write a social foundations–oriented theory paper that was so excellent that he would count it as a "pass" on the examination. He would read the paper, give feedback, and suggest rewrites. To my knowledge, no student had achieved what he considered to be an acceptable paper. A friend of mine, Tom Romberg, a math educator (subsequently on the University of Wisconsin faculty), and I decided to accept the challenge jointly. We had been reading about cybernetics and had been particularly inspired on this topic by the writings of Norbert Weiner and by personal discussions with Fred McDonald, an educational psychology professor. And so we wrote, and rewrote, and rewrote "A Cybernetic Model of Society." To no avail. "Very, very good, but no cigar."

The exam depicted a particular social issue and asked for an analysis, including appropriate citations from the theoretical literature. We both responded to the question citing one source: various aspects of "A Cybernetic Model of Society," by Alkin and Romberg. We passed with flying colors.

The evaluation message? Think outside the box and don't be afraid to take reasonable risks. Another sidelight to this story is the way that this interest in cybernetics introduced me to the complexity and interrelatedness of systems and the role of feedback in system change. In fact, the first publication I wrote that had the word *evaluation* in it (5 or 6 years later) was titled "Towards an Evaluation Model: A Systems Approach." I didn't continue writing about this topic, but it was and is implicit in my thinking about evaluation.

NEW DIRECTIONS FOR EVALUATION • DOI: 10.1002/ev

A Lucky Bounce

Those were some of the bunts, sacrifices, and bloop singles. Now let's turn to a "lucky bounce." So I was hired at UCLA in school administration. At about that time, 1965, the U.S. Department of Education was carrying on competitions for nationally sponsored Research and Development Centers. Our dean became frustrated with the year and a half effort by a committee of distinguished full professors to develop a proposal. Mired in their own self-interests, they never got started because they couldn't agree on a focus for the center. Dean Howard Wilson dismissed the committee and appointed a group of beginning assistant professors (me among them) chaired by a first-year associate professor, and told us to "write a winning proposal that capitalizes on the strengths of the department and not your own self-interests." We focused on evaluation, though no one on our faculty had done anything specifically related to that area. Evaluation was an encompassing topic that capitalized on a broad range of faculty expertise—sociologists, psychologists, methodologists, and others all fit in. We presented the proposal to the dean, who, noticing that no director had been included, told the beginning associate professor (a learning psychologist) that he was the director. When he objected, saying that he was not a good administrator, the dean turned to me and said, "Marv is the associate director." Thus, began my evaluation career (not quite). We got funded, primarily because the two sets of simulated site visits and debriefings that I organized made it look like this disparate group of prominent scholars knew each others' work, fit together, and would contribute something unique to evaluation understanding. (My background in simulations and role-playing entered yet again.)

I was satisfied with this new administrative assignment that had just been thrust upon me because it provided me with funding and I did, after all, have the opportunity to do some work on benefit/cost and cost effectiveness kinds of things. I was still well within my "comfort zone."

A Bloop Single

After serving 2 years as associate director, but really managing the Center for the Study of Evaluation (CSE) because of the absence or noninterest of the director, I had had it, and the U.S. Department of Education wanted a clearer management scheme. The dean tried but was unsuccessful at getting Ben Bloom to be director. He turned to me, saying that he thought I "could do the job." I asked him, "What in the hell do you think I've been doing for 2 years?" Angered and filled with the arrogance of a newly promoted associate professor, I indicated that I would talk only with the associate dean. After subsequent negotiations, I agreed to become the director of the CSE. In my mind, this meant that I really had to get serious about understanding what evaluation was and to begin taking a role in shaping the field.

And now we return to the "information for administrative decision making" theme. What better way to start seriously thinking about evaluation than this? One of the first studies I conducted was entitled "Evaluation and Decision Making: The Title VII Experience" (Alkin, Kosecoff, Fitz-Gibbon, & Seligman, 1974). What became clear to me in this study was that evaluation's impact extended beyond decision making. There were other kinds of ways in which evaluation had influence, had use. Thus, began for me a series of studies (e.g., "Using Evaluations," Alkin, Daillak, & White, 1979) and a multiyear focus on evaluation utilization. I, along with other early "use scholars"—Weiss, Patton, King, and Newman/Braskamp/Brown jointly—were part of what Mel Mark called "the golden age of evaluation research." My evaluation utilization research has been a guiding element in my subsequent thinking about evaluation.

Some Base Running

In putting together the AEA meeting symposium where an earlier version of this paper originated, David Williams was particularly struck by an example that I had given in the first chapter of my *Evaluation Essentials* book (Alkin, 2011). In that text, I described the process that my wife and I went through in selecting a house to purchase. In essence, in this "amateur" evaluation we selected criteria that we felt were important, then we provided a basis for attaching values or weightings for each and determined the maximum number of points that might be allocated to each dimension. We *actually* used this schema to come to a conclusion about which of three houses to purchase.

This may sound like I had become a Scriven evaluation acolyte. In fact, this example of "amateur evaluation" is NOT how I conduct my professional evaluations. I do not accept the role of evaluator as valuing agent. In the above example, my wife and I were simultaneously the users and the evaluators; thus, when we established criteria for judgment and a valuing scheme with weightings to criteria, a priori, we were doing so as stakeholders, potential users of the evaluation.

This does have some similarity to the way that I actually conduct evaluations (and thus is an element in my "prescriptive" model of evaluation). I work mostly doing formative and summary formative evaluations. In fact, I think that there are very few evaluations that truly are summative. Comparison programs are usually not available or necessary. In this situation, I work with potential users to engage in a priori valuing. In essence I engage stakeholders in identifying questions on which the evaluators should focus, the criteria for determining success, and the schema for valuing. I describe this procedure fully in Alkin (2011).

A Single

The National Society for the Study of Education devoted its 1991 yearbook to the topic *Evaluation and Education: At Quarter Century*. In essence, they asked early evaluation writers to comment on how their views of evaluation had changed in 25 years. In my chapter (Alkin, 1991), focused most specifically on an earlier paper in a volume by Carol Weiss (Alkin, 1972), I discussed modification of my views on evaluation in that period of time in the context of what I called "change influences." Among these was "influence of one's own research." I've already commented on this. My extensive research on evaluation utilization has helped to position where I am as an evaluator.

Another influence was field-based experiences—what I learned from doing literally hundreds of extensive evaluations. This work in formal education took place in local, state, and national governments, including various types of programs. Also I benefited from performing evaluations in many other settings: agricultural extension programs in multiple countries, a psychiatric resident training program, a program focusing on campesino entitlement in Ecuador, and others. One thing that became very clear to me was that context matters. Context influences. Evaluators have to be acutely conscious of context.

I also mentioned as a change influence the way in which one's theory is categorized by others. I imagine that I objected to the staid and mechanistic way that my earlier views were presented in category systems. This led me to consider the personal aspects of evaluation and to incorporate these into my evaluation writing.

Perhaps more important, the examination of these category systems led me to consider more thoughtfully the differences among evaluation theoretical perspectives—comparative evaluation theory. This, of course, eventuated in the evaluation theory tree and the two *Evaluation Roots* books (Alkin, 2004, 2013).

Finally, I mentioned a group of influences associated with one's professional colleagues. Included in this category was exposure to the views presented by other theorists and personal interactions with them. My views were shaped in important ways by professional colleagues and by my students. All of these contributed to my current evaluation understandings.

Lots of bunts, singles, etc. And so this short listing of hits, bunts, and so on, provides some insight into how I became my particular brand of evaluator.

References

Alkin, M. (1972). Evaluation theory development. In C. Weiss (Ed.), *Evaluating action programs*. Boston, MA: Allyn and Bacon. [Reprinted from Alkin, M. (1969). Evaluation theory development. *Evaluation Comment, 2*(1), 2–7].

Alkin, M. (1991). Evaluation theory development II. In M. McLaughlin & D. Phillips (Eds.), *Evaluation and education: At quarter century* (90th yearbook of the National Society for the Study of Education). Chicago, IL: University of Chicago Press.

Alkin, M. (2004). *Evaluation roots* (1st ed.). Thousand Oaks, CA: Sage Publications.

Alkin, M. (2011). *Evaluation essentials: From A to Z.* New York, NY: Guilford Press.

Alkin, M. (2013). *Evaluation roots* (2nd ed.). Thousand Oaks, CA: Sage Publications.

Alkin, M., & Christie, C. (2002). The use of role-play in teaching evaluation. *The American Journal of Evaluation, 23*(2), 209–219.

Alkin, M., Daillak, R., & White, P. (1979). *Using evaluations: Does evaluation make a difference? Sage Library of Social Research: Vol. 76.* Beverly Hills, CA: Sage Publications.

Alkin, M., Kosecoff, J., Fitz-Gibbon, C., & Seligman, R. (1974). *Evaluation and decision making: The Title VII experience (CSE Monograph Series in Evaluation, No. 4).* Los Angeles, CA: Center for the Study of Evaluation, UCLA.

MARVIN C. ALKIN is an emeritus professor in the Social Research Methodology Division of the Graduate School of Education and Information Studies at the University of California, Los Angeles.

NEW DIRECTIONS FOR EVALUATION • DOI: 10.1002/ev

Scriven, M. (2016). Thoughts about an early evaluation life. In D. D. Williams (Ed.), *Seven North American evaluation pioneers. New Directions for Evaluation, 150*, 33–39.

3

Thoughts About an Early Evaluation Life

Michael Scriven

Abstract

Scriven describes how he believes the early death of his father, constant intercontinental moving he experienced as a child, and associated fractures in relationships he began with peers influenced his "attitude towards the value of reason," which is his "main professional area of publication and evaluation." He recounts stories of developing his own evaluation life by running away from home at age 14 (following his father's example); writing an award-winning essay on quantitatively evaluating acts of valor (as he wanted to be a RAF pilot like his father); pursuing math, science, and philosophy in college; critiquing parapsychology; evaluating sports cars; exploring and teaching critical thinking; deciding where to go to university and where to work; and eventually being pulled into professional evaluation by being asked to work on a White House task force that included evaluating university courses and curricula on critical thinking; and collaborating with other early evaluation theorists. © 2016 Wiley Periodicals, Inc., and the American Evaluation Association.

Experiences in Evaluation

Okay, I'm going to have a shot at the best analysis I can give of my life's interest in evaluation. It should be treated as being obviously unreliable and probably invalid, and it's certainly embarrassing. I'm trying to do this, I suppose, in a very vague sense, as a test of what's possible objectively, or with lack of evidence, which is important for evaluators, so I'll try my best.

I was born in England and grew up there, raised in the conventional way. What was a little unusual about the way that I grew up was that beginning at age 12 months I moved. My mother moved me intercontinentally. That meant, in those days of course, 3 weeks in a ship each way, so it was a really substantial experience, but it went on throughout my life. I never spent more than 3 or 4 years in one continent. My mother was Australian, my father was an Air Force pilot in the British Isles, and so I used to vibrate between them and spent a bit more time in Australia when the war began.

I was treated badly because I was a kid in England, and the general way to bring up kids in England, in the middle class, was to send them to boarding school and other institutes away from home. I remember the day that I was left [at] boarding school—weeping pathetically, with the instructions to my parents from the headmaster lingering in my ears, which were, "We don't invite parents to visit for the first six months; it would upset the kids." Not a message that I was eager to hear that particular day.

Anyway, I spent several years there just before the war began. And my father died during those years. When war broke out, my mother's idea, sensibly enough, was to take my younger brother and me back to Australia, since we were eating English food and not contributing very much to the war efforts—the Allied Powers effort. And so we went to Australia, where I eventually went to university.

So that business of constant shifts meant absolute fracture of all friendships that lasted more than 2 or 3 years. And that meant you either survived without them or you didn't survive, so you survived without them. So that was the start that I think affected my attitude towards life to some degree and eventually my attitude toward the value of reason, which is my main professional area of publication and evaluation.

My father, who came from a working class family, was beat up by his father, and so he ran away from home when he was 14. I wasn't beat up by my mother, but she decided she wanted to take me out of my school and put me in a new one. When I was 14 it became clear to me that my mother's reasoning was no longer operating too well, and so I had to make a decision about whether to stay or go, and I decided to go. So I jumped off the train that was taking the three of us to another state, which stopped 600 miles away. So dropping off just as the train pulled out, I had the better part of a day before my mother could instigate any restraining activities, and she would then be in a rather bad position to do so from that distance. So I ran away. Boringly, I ran away to school; that is, I went back to the boys' school I was in, which I thought was a better place. So I never saw my parents after I was 14 or so.

At that age in those days one wasn't exactly well informed about clinical categorization. The fact that my mother was a paranoid schizophrenic, who was shortly afterwards hospitalized for the rest of her life, was something that didn't come clear to me. But what did become clear was the need to stand with my reasons and not with the affections. And I think that those experiences for me—the choice to go to school, having to run away from home when I was 14—forced a certain amount of independence on me. Every few years, I would be moved from England to Australia and then in the other direction, after being displayed to the grandparents. This had the rather unattractive result of breaking every friendship connection ever made. So that forced a certain amount of independence on me.

When I was 16, in 12th grade at my high school in Australia, my best subject was English. And there was a bequest at the school, which had been left for the best English essay written during the year. I decided to have a go at that—the Anderson essay competition. You could choose any topic you liked. The topic I chose, which is why I have found my interest in evaluation is lifelong, was rather peculiar. It was whether one could quantitatively evaluate acts of valor or heroism during the war in the process of awarding medals. That was affected by my orientation toward my father's career and my fixation on being a fighter pilot. My father was a fighter pilot in the RAF, and I had planned to become a senior officer in the RAF and a fighter pilot too.

At any rate, I spent a great deal of time that year writing this essay. It was a last effort I made at quantification of the concept of valor, though I've been rather favorably inclined toward qualitative approaches ever since. I won a prize for that essay, which inherited the idea that I was trying to develop mathematics in a way that follows ethics.

I didn't very much like mathematics, but that's what you had to have in order to get into navigation school. But as much as I wanted to get into the Air Force, they inconveniently stopped the war, and they were rather overstocked with pilots the next day. So they closed down the training school, which unfortunately left me in the latter half of the 12th grade with absolutely no preparation for any alternative pattern in life.

For survival, I had to go to college to fill in the gap in my life, which I had never intended to do. Since I'd been taking all the math and science classes in order to do well in navigation training school in the Air Force, I had no option other than to major in math and physics, and I had to go to university and do mathematics because there wasn't anything else I knew anything about.

I wasn't terribly good at math, but I got two degrees in it, and I always had a good deal of affection for it. I was a math major, but my instincts toward more of a humanities orientation were sort of knocking at the door, and now that my planned vocational opportunities were gone, I had to start thinking about other things. So I started doing some intern work as a mathematician. But I also started looking at math logic, because that was a step toward the more philosophical things that I was fiddling around with when I wrote the Anderson essay.

NEW DIRECTIONS FOR EVALUATION • DOI: 10.1002/ev

I was getting interested in questions for their own sake and got interested in philosophy because I was really interested in the foundations of mathematics. And I worked as an applied mathematician for a while, but I really was getting more and more interested in the mathematical foundations of philosophy and logic.

In school I had started to get the idea that philosophy was interesting, because a year or 2 years ahead of me there was a twelfth grader who was sort of famous. And he was famous because it was widely said that he had read all of Bertrand Russell. This was David Armstrong, who went on to become the philosophy guru at the University of Sydney and a famous philosopher, in Australia at least. It always impressed me that somebody who was just a high schooler, like me, was reading serious philosophy.

Then something interesting happened. A math teacher turned up at my school, which was called Geelong Grammar, where the king and queen sent Prince Charles. The math teacher was interesting: He was a priest in a Church of England Anglican school. He was coming out from England, where he had been a math student at Cambridge and had done very well in the math specialty program there. But that had been 15 or 20 years earlier; he was middle-aged at this point. He had come out because the Bishop of Queensland had selected him to be the headmaster of the main Anglican school in Queensland. But the bishop had made some mistake in writing to him and given the wrong date. So he arrived in Australia a year early. So the Bishop of Queensland called up these headmasters, including ours, and said, "Could you use a math teacher for a year?" and it turned out we could.

So the 12th grade math specialists, who were a fairly small class, were assigned to be specially tutored by him. And he turned out to be a very good mathematician, and quite inspiring. But he also, of course, because of his ecclesiastical training, was pretty well educated in philosophy. And I got interested in talking to him about the existence of God, which I was pretty skeptical about, but that became interesting. And then he lent me some books, including Kant's *Critique of Pure Reason*. And so I struggled through that.

Then when I got to the university I signed up in the advanced math program, which is what I spent my time on. But I also had one optional course, and so I went to see the chair of the philosophy department, and I said, "I'm really interested in taking some course where I could learn some more about philosophy, but I really don't want to begin at the beginning because I've done a bit of reading." And he said, "What reading have you done?" So I said, "Kant's *Critique*." And he said, "Ah, okay, I'll put you in the Kant course," which was the senior course. So I was in this group of eight or ten people who had spent many years doing philosophy, and that was quite interesting.

What I finished up doing, apart from sitting in on that philosophy course, was taking a logic course from someone else: a very good, practical logician, a student of Wittgenstein's who had come back from Cambridge imbued with the new philosophy of Wittgenstein, which was sweeping the philosophical world at that time. And I got very interested in logic other than mathematical logic. Eventually I decided I'd do my master's degree on the foundations of mathematics, which served as a joint degree, and that got me interested in the foundations of philosophy. I did a thesis on the scope and limitations of mathematical logic. So that was the beginning of my interest in method studies, the study of how much a subject could extend its boundaries or could not extend its boundaries.

So at the end of 4 years in college, I had two degrees: one in math and one in combined philosophy and math. So I was getting close to the applied logic area, which eventually got me into evaluation. And when I went up to university, I got involved with contemporary politics and a lot of other usual activities of kids in their undergraduate careers there.

I was particularly interested in parapsychology. I got interested in that partly because I had been brought up by my mother as a Christian Scientist, which was one of the fringe areas in parapsychology. And so I was interested in this, in reading quite a lot about it. I finally decided to do something about it, so I founded a student society. In those days it wasn't called a student society. It was the Melbourne University Society for Parapsychological Research. And we had some very good people in it. I had the use of the meeting rooms, and so I included a couple of senior researchers on the faculty of the physics department who also had interests in these paranormal phenomena. J. B. Rhine was the great guru of the field at Duke University. So we started with quite a lot of notoriety by getting in touch with the ABC, which is the Australian Broadcasting Commission, the BBC in Australia. And we went on the air, calling for people who had stories about mysterious things that we could investigate seriously.

We did some pretty serious investigation, and we found a couple of people who did a stage telepathy act—a very sophisticated one, a very impressive one. And given that they were looking pretty good, though I didn't know whether to believe them or not, I wrote to Rhine and said, "How about joining us in an experiment in which you run some card packs at Duke, and our subjects here will attempt to guess the order of the cards?" So we had this international experiment running, using these two guys, actually a man and his wife, the Piddingtons. And all we did was record what they were calling, and then we compared their calls with what the cards had actually been. And they weren't scoring high. But they were putting on a terrific act on the stage. So my conclusion was that they've got some very clever way of passing signals to each other that we haven't detected yet. This was all good training towards good critical thinking—applying the scientific method to new fields.

I finished college classes in Australia and went to Oxford to study philosophy. At the time, you went to Cambridge for physical science and Oxford for everything else, because there were only two philosophy faculty positions at Cambridge and there were 73 at Oxford. So that seemed the best option. I went there for a PhD in explanation theory. And again I tried to learn something about the limits of systems, systems of thought, and attempts to formalize particular logical function explanations.

After I got through the necessary 2 years' residence at Oxford, I had developed a healthy interest in sports cars, and at that time you couldn't buy them unless you had enough money to do it on the black market, so I looked for a job in America where you *could* buy sports cars, which brought me to the University of Minnesota.

I got a job via correspondence with the University of Minnesota. And one of the first things I did was get in touch with Rhine and go down to Duke and start talking to the gang down there. There was a very high-quality telepathy experiment going, with no fakery that anybody could find, and it was open for observation by other people. He had a couple of very good subjects who were scoring pretty well, at least to begin with, but they declined after a while. Anyway, I became pretty good friends with that group down there. And so I kept that up.

I was getting more and more interested in the limits of systems and the extent to which one could begin to learn something about whether their appearance really established what was needed to establish in mathematics, et cetera. So I got into these areas of science and philosophy of mathematics. And I began to get interested in critical thinking. It seemed like a more useful thing to learn and do than math logic, which was really a form of chess: It was fun but not very useful, although it has certainty, which was interesting. There was no such thing as computer science at this point. But there was a mathematical logic, which was used for programming language. So I found myself sitting in my office, when I was teaching a class at the University of Minnesota, being visited by a steady stream of recruiters from a big computer company looking for students of mine who could then embark on the processes of looking at programming logic.

Meanwhile, I was teaching critical thinking and other philosophy courses, but I was particularly interested in critical thinking. And things were going on in the wider world of education that eventually became the business of Sputnik and associated reforms in the science curriculum to match the Russians' efforts. And once that was going, the White House felt that it was under some pressure to reform the social studies as well. And so it set about building a committee to head the enterprise of reforming the social studies. They set up a group for social science innovation. And I was asked if I would join that as the representative for critical thinking, which was sort of a fringe area of the social studies. I was pulled in order to represent the teaching of critical thinking in the social studies area. I was on the White House task force doing that for several years; it had quite a bit of funding.

I got more and more interested in looking at the following question: In the several hundred critical thinking courses in reputable universities in the United States, is there any evidence that it does any good? It turned out that there wasn't anything worthwhile. So I started into the business of trying to get more serious about what it would take to establish superior critical thinking skills, in the way of tests and curriculum that would test that appropriately. And as a result, I got into the beginning of evaluation, because I found there were actually people working on evaluating education in a serious way. And so I started looking at what they were doing.

My very last point: Not many people in the social studies had any capacity for either doing serious critical thinking or teaching it. So that was the beginning of progress. I was now really evaluating the teaching of critical thinking, interested in the question of who could do it well. In fact, nobody knew much; there wasn't any experienced approach to evaluating it. I thought that I could surely do a little better and started working on a systematic study of comparison groups that we'd run through different approaches to teaching critical thinking.

So that's how I got into the evaluation business and started reading what people were beginning to write. Dan Stufflebeam and colleagues of his wrote papers on evaluation and were beginning to get some reactions to their work. I came to an American Educational Research Association meeting where people were talking about evaluation and was very kindly treated by Dan Stufflebeam and other people who really knew something about the subject, and I really appreciated talking to them about evaluation from that point on.

MICHAEL SCRIVEN is a professor of psychology at Claremont Graduate University and co-director of the Claremont Evaluation Center.

NEW DIRECTIONS FOR EVALUATION • DOI: 10.1002/ev

Stufflebeam, D. L. (2016). Factors that influenced my conduct of evaluations and evaluation training programs. In D. D. Williams (Ed.), *Seven North American evaluation pioneers. New Directions for Evaluation, 150,* 41–49.

4

Factors That Influenced My Conduct of Evaluations and Evaluation Training Programs

Daniel L. Stufflebeam

Abstract

In stories he shares about his own evaluation life, Stufflebeam notes some of the fundamental values he learned from his parents' examples and efforts to help him develop these values as a child growing up during the Depression. He also shares a story about his extraprofessional evaluation experiences as a substitute teacher in Chicago, where he taught in more than 40 different schools and observed the need for professional evaluation of the school system. He lists many other extraprofessional evaluation experiences and connects them to his decades of developing the context, inputs, processes, and products (CIPP) approach and his professional evaluation practices. © 2016 Wiley Periodicals, Inc., and the American Evaluation Association.

Experiences in Evaluation

I appreciate the opportunity to participate in Dr. Williams' examination of why certain evaluation theorists conceptualize, write about, and practice evaluation as they do. During my career I have been privileged to conduct evaluations with some of the evaluation field's most prolific contributors. Among others, they include Ralph Tyler, Egon Guba, Robert Stake, Michael Scriven, Ernie House, and Elliott Eisner. No doubt my evaluation approach and practices owe much to lessons learned while inter-acting and working with these incredibly dedicated and talented colleagues.

In several publications I have described and analyzed these theorists' backgrounds and contributions (Stufflebeam & Coryn, 2014; Stufflebeam, Madaus, & Kellaghan, 2000; Stufflebeam & Shinkfield, 2007). For this ar-ticle, Dr. Williams asked me to reflect and report similarly on my own con-tributions, including, especially, early experiences that helped shape my evaluation-related contributions. I assume he had in mind particularly the CIPP Evaluation Model, the Joint Committee standards for evaluations, and the evaluation doctoral programs I have developed and led. Briefly, the CIPP Model (see Chapter 15 in Stufflebeam & Shinkfield, 2007; also Chapter 13 in Stufflebeam & Coryn, 2014) calls for formative and summative evalua-tions of a program's context, inputs, processes, and products (CIPP). The Joint Committee (Joint Committee on Standards for Educational Evalua-tion, 1981, 1988, 1994, 2009, 2010) standards require evaluations to be useful, feasible, ethical, accurate, and accountable. And the PhD programs I developed and led were the Western Michigan University Interdisciplinary PhD Program in Evaluation (see Coryn, Stufflebeam, Davidson, & Scriven, 2010; Stufflebeam, 2001) and an earlier similar program at The Ohio State University.

Summary and Analysis of Experiences That Influenced My Evaluation Work

A handout chart created for presentation at the American Evaluation As-sociation meeting in 2013 (see handout for session 928 at Williams, 2013) summarizes how, over nearly 50 years, a fairly wide range of personal and professional experiences helped shape my theory for and practice of eval-uation. The chart displays a five by three matrix. Its five row headings are family background, education, cultural and political environment, key eval-uation experiences, and influential persons. The three column headings are areas of influence, examples of influence, and manifestation in one's con-cept of evaluation. Print space limitations for this article preclude displaying and explaining the chart's contents here. I hope readers who download and study the chart will find it useful for understanding the range of experiences that have shaped my ideas about and practice of evaluation.

To round out this article, I share a couple of early life experiences that profoundly influenced my thinking about and practice of evaluation. My ap-proach to program evaluation addresses two areas: (1) the conduct of evalu-ations (standards for sound evaluations; stakeholder engagement; planning, budgeting, contracting, and administering evaluations; collecting, analyz-ing, synthesizing, and reporting information; fostering use of findings; and meta-evaluation), and (2) the development of competent evaluators and evaluation-oriented leaders/evaluation clients. The remainder of this arti-cle relates two stories from my early development that helped shape how

I conduct evaluations and how I have trained and mentored evaluation specialists and evaluation-oriented leaders.

Story 1

This experience helped shape my development of the CIPP Evaluation Model. As best I can recall, creation of the CIPP Model began in 1961 in the Chicago Public Schools. In 1960, upon my release from active duty in the U.S. Army, I had moved to Chicago, where my wife was teaching in the Chicago Public Schools. In January of 1961, I entered Loyola University's graduate program, took a full load of courses, which were delivered at night, and for my daytime activity worked on Tuesdays and Thursdays as a graduate research assistant to Loyola's dean of education, Dr. John Wozniak. Since I was free during daytime hours on Mondays, Wednesdays, and Fridays, I used those times to serve as a substitute teacher in the Chicago schools. Because I could not teach on adjacent days, the district regularly sent me to a different school for every assignment. Most of the schools were in poverty-stricken neighborhoods.

As a former teacher from rural, relatively tranquil Iowa, I was astonished by what I observed in over 40 Chicago schools. Most of the teachers were substitutes like I was, except they regularly served in the same school every day. Many schools had no books because funds for books had to come from the school's broken window fund, which was depleted. Gangs were prevalent, violence was a common occurrence, two armed policemen patrolled the halls in most of the schools, student attendance was low, teacher and student turnover during the course of a semester often approached or exceeded 100%, and the drug culture was rampant in surrounding neighborhoods. In many cases students and teachers spoke different languages. This was especially prevalent due to the recent Hungarian Revolution and associated influx to Chicago of many Hungarian refugees. Many teachers I encountered in school cafeterias or break rooms seemed to be jaded, cynical, or depressed. My main assignment typically was to keep order, not to try to teach. If you ever saw the movie *Blackboard Jungle*, I think you can get the picture.

After my first semester and one summer term at Loyola, I received a fellowship to attend Purdue University. In one of my first courses at Purdue, students were assigned to write about some personal experience in education. For my paper, I chose to address the need for evaluation in Chicago's public schools. Because I'd had to substitute in a different school for almost every assignment, I concluded I might be the only person who knew how bad things were across the district, especially in the inner city schools. Otherwise, how could the district accept and continue with the status quo?

To make a long story short, it was then that I wrote about the need for context evaluations. Some years later, after Ohio State's John Ramseyer had channeled me into the evaluation business, I drew on my Chicago substitute teaching experience to include context evaluation as a part of the evaluation model I was developing for use by Ohio's school districts. That model became known as the CIPP Model (Stufflebeam et al., 1971), with the C in the acronym CIPP standing for context evaluation. A context evaluation assesses needs, problems, assets, and opportunities as a basis for determining and assessing goals and priorities. Building on a conviction that evaluation basically should be a force for improvement, I added input evaluation (I) to help assure that sound program plans would be generated, process evaluation (P) to guide implementation of plans, and product evaluation (P) to help assure that programs would be effective in producing sound outcomes.

Story 2

Experiences have helped shape my training and mentoring of evaluators and evaluation-oriented leaders. In pondering why I have conceived and delivered evaluation training as I have, I was reminded of how my family toughed it out through depression years (1935 on into the 1940s). While rejecting any idea of seeking or accepting public welfare, my mom and dad overcame many obstacles, climbed up life's ladder of success themselves, and gave my sisters and me the valuable grounding in moral, spiritual, and democratic principles, plus hard work, that propelled us to also ascend several rungs of life's ladder of success. When I consider the very good conditions under which my children and grandchildren have grown up, it is hard to recall that the circumstances of my early years were so different.

When I was a young child, aged around five, my family was what today would be termed "under the poverty line"; in fact, by today's standards we were way under the poverty line. My mom and dad were struggling to pay off the $800 cost of our old drafty house, with Dad chopping wood for a dollar a day. We had no public welfare assistance and didn't want any. We were blessed with what we needed: each other, supportive neighbors and extended family, a roof over our heads, an acre on which to grow our food, our church, effective public schools, a nation of liberty and opportunity, and more.

Our house was located in rural Iowa, where winter temperatures often stayed well below zero for weeks. We had no running water, no indoor plumbing, no central heating, and no electrical appliances. After four of us had emergency appendectomies, our dug well was found to be polluted—probably from the stockyards just across the road and railroad tracks from our house. Dad and Grandpa subsequently dug, with hand shovels, a six-feet-deep trench over 100 yards long so they could hook us up to city water.

We kept food cold in our icebox with blocks of ice, which we got off a rickety delivery truck about once a week. We raised almost everything we ate, including vegetables, fruits, and chickens, and each day I walked to a farm down the road to retrieve a pail of fresh milk. During the autumn months, Mom canned much of what we would eat during the winter, and Dad drove to St. Ansgar, Iowa in our old 1934 Ford, with the back seats removed to bring back 800 pounds of potatoes to help get us through the winter.

For warmth in the cold winters, we huddled near a pot-bellied stove (nearly burning on one side and freezing on the other) and at night slept under heavy patchwork quilts. Often mornings would find a layer of snow on the quilts from the night's passing blizzard, which had blown right through gaps around the windows of our house. For fuel, my dad and grandpa regularly walked the nearby railroad tracks to pick up, bag, and bring back coal left by the daily passing of locomotive-powered hog and cattle trains (whose smoke often darkened Mom's laundry that was hanging on the clothesline). When I was a little older, I regularly walked the tracks during hunting season to shoot rabbits, squirrels, and pheasants for our table.

For fun, my sisters and I were occasionally regaled with poems by the king of hobos when he stopped by our house to ask for food. His name was Hairbreadth Harry. One poem I recall was "Hairbreadth Harry is no fairy; he can neither flit nor fly; Hairbreadth Harry is no fairy; he must eat like you or I; he must eat or he will die." We would giggle and go ask Mom to give our hobo friend some bread.

I took care of our chickens, and on Saturdays Dad would send me with a hatchet to catch and kill a chicken for Sunday's customary fried chicken dinner. After the chicken was dipped in scalding water, I hung it by its feet, plucked its feathers, used flaming brown paper bags to singe off its pin feathers, and delivered it to Mom for cleaning, separating parts, and frying on Sunday. I don't like chicken any more because what one gets these days in supermarkets and restaurants is grossly inferior to the fried chicken I enjoyed as a child.

My mom sewed from whole cloth my shirts and overalls and my sisters' dresses. Mom was a great seamstress. Our family was blessed with spiritual and educational benefits by regularly attending church services—usually four or five times a week. If I ever learned how to debate, it was in that Baptist church's Bible study meetings.

Eventually, Dad got a good job at John Deere Tractor Company in Waterloo and worked there for 33 years. Ultimately, he advanced to his favorite position of operating a dynamometer to measure and document performance characteristics of each diesel engine as it came off the production line. One time he remarked that he was amazed that even after their standardized production some engines were clearly superior to the others.

With our improved financial status, we moved next door into a big better house, which during the 1800s had been a hotel on a stagecoach line. We kept ownership of our previous house and its adjoining acre of ground, and Mom rented that house to a young family with children. Mom also rented our "new" house's extra bedrooms to persons passing through or working in town, and I became proficient in operating our Speed Queen mangle to iron sheets for Mom's rental business. I slept in one of the six upstairs bedrooms, and Mom rented the other five for $3 a day or $15 a week. One time reputed mobster Mickey Cohen and his young son—on their way to Las Vegas—stayed overnight in one of our tourist rooms. Other renters included members of the New York Philharmonic Orchestra, who were playing a concert at nearby Wartburg College; the head auctioneer of the North American continent's largest annual horse sale, which is located on the outskirts of our town, Waverly; a number of Wartburg College co-eds; an FBI agent who frequently appeared to investigate something that he kept secret; and a United Methodist Church bishop and his wife, who for about 10 years spent their annual summer vacations in our house. Contacts with such renters surely enriched my perspective on the larger world outside my hometown.

Mom had attended the local Wartburg College for only 2 years because it closed (for about 5 years) in 1933 due to the Great Depression. She regretted very much that she couldn't attend the additional 2 years required to earn her degree. As my sisters and I grew older, Mom urged all of us to attend an accredited college. As soon as we graduated high school, we all attended college. Moreover, we all worked part-time jobs during fall and winter semesters and full-time jobs during summers to pay our way through school.

My sisters and I had a very happy childhood and never could have believed that by future standards we would have been termed "poor." Instead, all three of us very much appreciated the richly rewarding childhood our parents had provided for us.

Relevance of Story 2 to My Approach to Evaluation. So what does the above story have to do with the ways I conduct my evaluation work? In general, I think it suggests how so-called poverty, coupled with solid family values and growth through problem solving and reflection, can provide a foundation for one's educational and social development, assumption of individual responsibility, proclivity to work hard, commitment to high standards of performance, and orientation to help others in need.

As I have thought about the story of my childhood, it has occurred to me that the challenging circumstances of my earliest years and my subsequent rise out of so-called poverty influenced me not only to take responsibility for my own educational and professional development, but also to deliver experience-based graduate education to my students.

I strongly believe that the school of hard knocks can be a pretty good teacher. Maybe the "hard times" of my early childhood help explain why in directing evaluation doctoral programs I always required my doctoral advisees to start at the bottom of an evaluation career ladder and ascend it by conducting a succession of increasingly challenging and educationally rewarding evaluation tasks throughout their graduate programs. I arranged for each of my doctoral majors to start with the very mundane tasks in evaluation work: for example, copying, collating, and stapling evaluation instruments and other materials; handling mailing of survey instruments; retrieving completed instruments; cleaning and coding data responses; setting up conference rooms, sweeping floors (if needed); and keeping office equipment in working order.

Subsequent tasks for these students have included serving a particular role in an evaluation. These roles could entail such tasks as scheduling site visits, interviewing, observing, analyzing data, drafting reports, preparing briefing sheets, supporting site visit teams, and so on. Before a doctoral student left the program, either prior to graduation or in the year or two after, I typically arranged for her or him to direct a nationally significant evaluation. Such evaluation projects included responding to requests for proposals, contracting with the federal government or a foundation, and hiring as consultants or evaluation team members such evaluation icons as Gene Glass, Robert Stake, Michael Scriven, Lee Cronbach, William Gephart, William Webster, James Jacobs, Carl Candoli, Jason Millman, Ralph Tyler, Robert Ingle, Egon Guba, George Madaus, Roald Campbell, William Michaels, Jack Taylor, Malcolm Provus, Richard Jaeger, and Francis Chase.

The top step on the evaluator doctorate development ladder was oriented to introducing the student to the evaluation field's best and brightest scholars and practitioners and demonstrating to such future colleagues the student's evaluation skills, management proficiency, and potential for evaluation leadership. Students who climbed the evaluation career ladder under my direction included such contributors to evaluation and evaluation-oriented leadership as James Adams, Diane Reinhard, Howard Merriman, Jerry Walker, Robert Rodosky, Tom Owens, David Nevo, Darrell Root, Gary Wegenke, Lori Wingate, Carl Hanssen, John Evers, Tony Shinkfield, Jeri Nowakowski, Allan Nowakowski, Tanya Suarez, Blaine Worthen, Michael Hock, Sharon Dodson, Sandra Ryan, and others.

Harkening back to the biblical training of my youth and the importance of such doctrines as the Ten Commandments and the U.S. Bill of Rights, I have always believed that professional services such as evaluation should be grounded in pertinent moral and ethical principles. Accordingly, I have included professional standards for evaluations not only as bases for evaluation plans and practices but as foundational content for evaluation training programs.

I have also subscribed to an objectivist, as opposed to relativist, orientation to evaluation. Although ironclad conclusions about a program's merit may be difficult or beyond one's capacity to determine, I believe evaluators should do their best to search for firm, valid conclusions and then exercise appropriate circumspection in reporting those conclusions. For me, it would be a cop-out to conclude that a program's merit is only in the eyes of different beholders and could legitimately be judged good or bad depending on who is doing the judging. I agree with the sentiment Harry Truman expressed when he said he was looking for a one-armed

NEW DIRECTIONS FOR EVALUATION • DOI: 10.1002/ev

economist because he was tired of receiving equivocal reports about the U.S. economy couched in the expressions "on the one hand ... but on the other hand ... " Experience has taught me that decision makers will not long seek and value evaluation services that report multiple and often contradictory conclusions and stop short of presenting the best available interpretation with its appropriate cautions.

Above I have made several references to evaluation-oriented leaders, because that is a critical part of my concept of evaluation and of my approach to evaluation training. An evaluation-oriented leader is a decision maker who understands basic evaluation concepts and is proficient in and committed to the use of systematic evaluation to guide decision making and meet accountability requirements. In the evaluation doctoral programs I have led, I have regularly engaged both future administrators and future evaluation specialists to learn evaluation theory and methods together and especially to collaborate in conducting evaluations. The payoff for evaluators of such co-learning has been that the administrative colleagues typically help the evaluation specialists plan and conduct studies that are practical and relevant to program needs. Part of the payoff for the future administrators is that experience in working with evaluation specialists helps them overcome any propensity to be intimidated by supposed evaluation technocrats who are steeped in the mysteries of statistics and research design. The glue for obtaining an effective, symbiotic relationship between evaluation specialists and evaluation-oriented leaders is in getting both parties to work together in learning and applying standards of the evaluation field.

Closing

Over the years I believe that basically all of my efforts to conceptualize evaluation have been drawn from reflections on real-world experiences. Moreover, the PhD programs I have developed and led were firmly grounded in a learning-by-doing approach and in the standards of the field.

In conclusion, I think it is useful to reflect on and examine the bases for different evaluation approaches. Such reflection and examination can help one understand alternative approaches, judge their soundness and applicability, and identify ways to strengthen them. As noted above, my experiences as a substitute teacher in Chicago inner-city schools helped shape my development of the CIPP Model, and my early life experiences during the Great Depression of the 1930s and the early 1940s no doubt influenced my later employment of an evaluation career ladder concept to direct evaluation doctoral programs.

As cryptic as this paper is, I hope that many evaluators and their clients will glean useful lessons from the preceding stories and the analyses in the handout at Williams (2013).

References

Coryn, C. L. S., Stufflebeam, D. L., Davidson, E. J., & Scriven, M. (2010). The interdisciplinary Ph.D. in Evaluation: Reflections on its development and first seven years. *Journal of MultiDisciplinary Evaluation*, 6(13), 118–129.

Joint Committee on Standards for Educational Evaluation (Daniel L. Stufflebeam, Chair). (1981). *Standards for evaluations of educational programs, projects, and materials*. New York: McGraw-Hill.

Joint Committee on Standards for Educational Evaluation (Daniel L. Stufflebeam, Chair). (1988). *The personnel evaluation standards: How to assess systems for evaluating educators*. Newbury Park, CA: Sage.

Joint Committee on Standards for Educational Evaluation (James R. Sanders, Chair). (1994). *The program evaluation standards* (2nd ed.). Thousand Oaks, CA: Sage.

Joint Committee on Standards for Educational Evaluation (Arlen Gullickson, Chair). (2009). *The personnel evaluation standards: How to assess systems for evaluating educators*. Thousand Oaks, CA: Sage.

Joint Committee on Standards for Educational Evaluation (D. B. Yarbrough, L. Shulha, R. K. Hopson, & F. A. Caruthers [Eds.]). (2010). *The program evaluation standards* (3rd ed.). Thousand Oaks, CA: Sage.

Stufflebeam, D. L. (2001). *Evaluation values and criteria checklist*. Retrieved from http://www.wmich.edu/evalctr/wp-content/uploads/2010/05/values_criteria.pdf

Stufflebeam, D. L., & Coryn, C. L. S. (2014). *Evaluation theory, models, & applications* (2nd ed.). San Francisco, CA: Jossey-Bass.

Stufflebeam, D. L., Foley, W. J., Gephart, W. J., Guba, E. G., Hammond, R. L., Merriman, H. O., & Provus, M. (1971). *Educational Evaluation and Decision Making*. Itasca, IL: Peacock.

Stufflebeam, D. L., Madaus, G. F., & Kellaghan, T. (2000). *Evaluation models: Viewpoints on educational and human services evaluation*. Boston, MA: Kluwer.

Stufflebeam, D. L., & Shinkfield, A. J. (2007). *Evaluation theory, models, and applications*. San Francisco, CA: Jossey-Bass.

Williams, D. D. (2013, October). *Themes from case studies of evaluators' lives*. Symposium organized and presented with Marv Alkin, Eleanor Chelimsky, Michael Patton, Robert Stake, Ernie House, Michael Scriven, and Daniel Stufflebeam at the annual American Evaluation Association meetings, Washington, DC. Retrieved from http://comm.eval.org/communities/community-home/librarydocuments/viewdocument?DocumentKey=7b1fd99f-53a1-45af-8557-261c038a5a04&CommunityKey=000000 00-0000-0000-0000-000000000000&tab=librarydocuments

DANIEL L. STUFFLEBEAM *was the founder and director of the Evaluation Center and is an emeritus professor at Western Michigan University.*

Chelimsky, E. (2016). Probing the past to understand the present: Can we relate early training and life experience to our evaluative orientations? In D. D. Williams (Ed.), *Seven North American evaluation pioneers. New Directions for Evaluation, 150*, 51–63.

5

Probing the Past to Understand the Present: Can We Relate Early Training and Life Experience to our Evaluative Orientations?

Eleanor Chelimsky

Abstract

Chelimsky shares her own stories about her evaluation life and comments on connections she sees between her extraprofessional and professional evaluation life experiences. These stories come from a paper she prepared for the American Evaluation Association 2013 symposium session, based in part on interviews conducted by David Williams. She mentions the influence her parents had on her values and her evaluation life. She elaborates on the influence she feels that her career in piano performance and her experiences living in Paris, France had on her evolving extraprofessional evaluation life and her professional evaluation experiences in her later career. © 2016 Wiley Periodicals, Inc., and the American Evaluation Association.

Early Experience and Evaluation

How do particular kinds of training and particular types of early experience affect the way we think about and conduct evaluations? To me, this is a difficult question to answer, in the sense that we are never fully conscious of how our brains work or how our memories and traumas move us one way or another in making decisions; nor is it easy to distinguish the roles played in our development—not only by training and experience, but also by inborn individual talents, specific circumstances, and just plain luck. Still it seems to me that if we leave ample room for plausible rival hypotheses and rely heavily on conscious references to earlier experience, we can't go too far wrong; and, of more consequence, the very process of examining these hidden trails of connection could have value for evaluators generally. Thus, looking carefully at early nonevaluative training and experience could make an important contribution to the efforts evaluators make to examine their own values.

In my own case—having had extensive musical training and having been a concert pianist in Europe before becoming an evaluator—I can now see, thanks to David Williams' prodding, that, although I had never thought about it before, there may indeed have been some substantial connections linking this combination of early training, concert experience, and life lived abroad with certain of my later assumptions and tendencies as an evaluator.

There are so many of these connections! My parents, for example, were big on rational decision making, and I was taught early on to try to envisage all potential costs and benefits when making choices. And although my parents were good about letting me make at least some decisions for myself, I always had to explain exactly how I came to make them. What were the pros and cons, especially the intangible ones? And what were the long-term results I was expecting (not just the likely ones but the unlikely ones as well)? So as I look at it from a "connections" point of view, my parents gave me a two-edged gift there—not only the habit of thinking about potential losses and longer-term gains, but also the confidence necessary to make decisions—which has certainly been useful to me in music as well as in evaluation. However, among the diversity of influences I've assimilated (from parents, peer groups, mentors, and all the myriad shapers of young minds), it seems to me that two aspects of my early experience are most closely connected to the way I've conceived and practiced evaluation. These are (a) musical training and performance, and (b) lessons learned as a consequence of living in Paris.

Influence of Musical Training and Concertizing

An Orientation Toward Synthesis

One thing that is basic to performing classical music, in addition to the normal analytical work involved in music study and learning, is the need for synthetic thinking. A musician must gracefully combine form and content (that is, convey both the musical form utilized by the composer—in a three-voice Bach fugue, say, or a Beethoven sonata—along with its melodic, harmonic, and rhythmic content), in such a way that the two are intimately and expressively integrated. But the style of the music (e.g., baroque, romantic, modern, postmodern) must also be integrated into that form and content, and the whole performance and program carefully considered from the viewpoint of its likely audience. Thus, a musician needs to think about and integrate into his or her playing what an audience, particularly the different components of that audience, might be expected to know, perceive, feel, and appreciate about an interpretation. Further, there is in music performance a three-way relationship of the composer's text, the artist's playing, and the audience's reactions that when thoughtfully applied more or less forces synthetic thinking by the performer.

Of course, this is not so different from evaluation. We have the same job of analysis in reaching an evaluative conclusion and also the same requirement for synthesis when integrating context, questions, methods, data, practitioner/participant experience, and user needs, as we try to say what happened in a program, how well it worked, or how our findings should be used. But evaluation requires a great deal more analysis than music, and most evaluators are trained in applications of particular methods that are so meticulous and detailed that they often overwhelm the processes of synthesis, of visualizing the "big picture," including the historical and political context or the system effects vis-à-vis other subject areas.

As a result, perhaps because musical training had driven me in this direction, I think I was always looking for the more perfect synthesis, constantly adding to the kinds of things that needed to be considered in an evaluation design: for example, collecting and synthesizing all relevant prior evaluation findings; reviewing the historical record and the political problems that are explicit or implicit in an evaluation question; looking at all stakeholder positions; assessing potential spillover into exogenous areas. Also I tried very hard when hiring evaluation staff to determine who thought analytically and who thought synthetically, in order to ensure that both types of thinking were present in our evaluation teams. Indeed, it took me a long time to figure out how to recognize these individual traits in an initial interview, and I usually ended up asking prospective staff how they would have dealt with a synthesis problem we had recently encountered in an evaluation (for example, how to think about and bring together the issues involved in improving home health care for the elderly). Similarly, for each of our studies I spent a lot of time thinking about what might be meaningful, important, and credible to our audience of different users but, as in music, without in any way compromising the essentials, the integrity, of the evaluation.

The Audience as Integral Component of Music and Evaluation

In a similar way, my thinking about evaluation users was influenced by the process I had gone through as a pianist, trying to work out what made a musical performance credible to the different kinds of people in a concert

audience and how (or whether) I should change an interpretation in consequence. At the Government Accountability Office (GAO), where I went in
1980 to establish an evaluation unit, we had many dissimilar users, including the relevant actors in the executive, legislative, and judicial branches
of government along with the GAO's own auditors. But these users were
no more dissimilar than the concert audiences I knew, made up of persons
from different backgrounds, different levels of musical knowledge, different national musical cultures. I had seen that a certain kind of traditional
Beethoven playing, for example, could be well respected in Stuttgart but
criticized as dry or formal in Paris or Milan. Within a single concert audience some listeners appreciated sophisticated nuances, while others were
oblivious; some loved innovative interpretations, but some were impatient
with the slightest deviation from the accepted standard. I realized that in
evaluation as in music (a) I needed to move away from the perspective of
the evaluation producer and consider much more carefully the perspective
of the evaluation user, and (b) there could be some danger in doing that. Just
as too much emphasis given to audience reactions at a concert can lessen
the pianist's reverence for the composer's intentions and transform a valid
interpretation into an effort at crowd pleasing, too much emphasis on user
credibility can cause evaluators to soften or lose entirely some important
lessons from their work.

I did three things at GAO that stem, I think, from this earlier musical experience as I endeavored to increase our persuasiveness to auditorial,
congressional, executive-branch, and Supreme Court users.

First, I developed a checklist for my own use in assessing the credibility
of our reports from a reader's viewpoint. Among other things, I included
T. S. Eliot's six criteria for quality in poetry, which acknowledge both the
need for integrity in the work and the need for persuasiveness directed at
the reader.

Second, before every congressional testimony I held what we called
"murder boards." All the staff who had worked on an evaluation would get
together, think about what could be most controversial among the findings,
and imagine what arguments might be raised against them, in what context,
and by whom. For example, we would look up the professional background
of everyone sitting on the relevant congressional committee to see how they
might react. When I was at GAO between 1980 and 1994, most members
of Congress were lawyers, but many came from backgrounds that were very
different; their political affiliations were different; their views of the public
interest—especially with regard to scope of government versus equality of
opportunity—were different; and some had much more of a state/local orientation than a federal or national one. These murder boards could reach
extremities because we were preparing to defend our work against anything
that might conceivably be asked, and staff would sometimes think up what
appeared to be quite preposterous questions. Yet no effort here was ever

wasted: Some of these questions actually did end up being posed at congressional hearings, and the exercise forced us to look at our reports from a user's point of view.

The third thing I did at GAO that involved integrating audiences into our evaluation concept was to try to produce evaluation reports that, although they couldn't be beautiful, glorious, or sublime (like music), were at least focused on the question, written with clarity, well organized in form, interesting in content, and pleasurable to read.

I was, of course, absurdly trying to imbue evaluation with some of the musical splendors lost in my past, and naturally that effort didn't often succeed. But when it did, we always recognized that success because we found evidence from the questions we received that the reports had, for once, been carefully read and understood by our audiences. A big difference between music and evaluation is that when you play a concert, the music you make may not be appreciated by everyone in the audience; but at least it's always heard. Evaluation reports, on the other hand, can be so repetitious, obscure, awkwardly phrased, and competently opposed by their political enemies that they are never read at all.

A Bias Toward Innovation

Despite a few conservative artists here and there, along with a great many ultraconservative patrons and audiences, innovation has always been one of the ways we've judged the quality of a work of art. Indeed, classical musicians are carefully trained to recognize the specific types of innovation that have characterized each composer, and few criticisms are more devastating to a musician than the adjective *derivative*. Wagner with his chromatic harmonies, Debussy with his transformative ninths, and Schoenberg with his 12-tone system are all exemplars of this musical attachment to innovation that marked my early training and that I brought with me to evaluation.

One particular aspect of evaluation that forces innovation is that practicing evaluators often find themselves in situations that have not been studied by theorists, so the very circumstances of their work oblige them to innovate. But this is different from music, where innovation is not just an order of business, but rather the hallmark of the composer or performing artist. So I see now that my training probably made innovation an article of faith for me and pushed me to take risks in evaluation that were not necessarily appreciated at GAO, where the traditionalism of the auditor could make change difficult. But like music, evaluation is an ongoing enterprise in which learning builds on learning. New kinds of evaluation questions, new appreciations of context-relevance, new understandings of the past all lead to new methods, mixed methods, greater inclusiveness, different areas of emphasis. At GAO, right from the beginning I found myself involved in developing new methods (e.g., the evaluation synthesis, the rapid examination of program operations and service delivery, the prospective evaluation synthesis, etc.) based on the nontraditional kinds of questions we were receiving from the Congress. Almost all of this innovation was entirely logical, I think, because it had for its object to increase our ability to answer these questions and to improve the methodological credibility of our findings. But the joy of it, for me, certainly came from some internal sense that innovation is, in and of itself, something to strive for.

In short, as I think back it seems to me that much of the evaluation work I did at NATO (the North Atlantic Treaty Organization), at the MITRE Corporation, and at GAO reflects the influence of early training in another field. But music is not the only influence I should talk about here. I lived in France for nearly 20 years (1948–1967), and there are two specific lessons I learned there that—among many, many others—deeply affected my approach to evaluation. The first was the discovery that a strong networking effort could have amazing effects on shaping public opinion and policy making; the second was that, no matter how excellent and exhaustive that networking effort might be, a single credible voice could demolish its achievements in the blink of an eye.

Influence of Living in Paris: The Power of Networking and the Courage to Speak Out

The Conventional French Wisdom About Freedom in the Soviet Union

Jean-Paul Sartre and Albert Camus had been heroes of mine since I read *The Age of Reason*, *The Plague*, and *The Stranger* in French class, long before leaving for France. To my adolescent mind, these two writer-philosophers were revered spokesmen for artistic freedom, individual liberty, and personal responsibility. But when I arrived in France in June of 1948, President Truman's Berlin airlift, which was intended to counter the Soviet blockade of Berlin, was just beginning and soon became the first hot political confrontation of the Cold War. Communism, not freedom, had become the major philosophical issue of the day in Paris, and both Sartre and Camus were now, as the reigning "philosophes engagés," solidly entrenched on the left, sharing the concerns of socialist ideas in France and providing leadership for them. Camus, as editor of the newspaper *Combat*, wrote editorials that everyone read; and Sartre was ubiquitous, holding forth at cafes in Saint-Germain-des-Pres, lecturing at open-air demonstrations, opining in Communist newspapers and magazines, and speaking out in his own journal, *Les Temps Modernes*. Little by little you could see some intense maneuvering and rallying taking place, fortified by myths about liberty in the Soviet Union dispensed by Louis Aragon and Ilya Ehrenburg that gradually took over more and more of public opinion in Paris. Yet there had been no lack of warnings about the realities of life in the Soviet Union.

NEW DIRECTIONS FOR EVALUATION • DOI: 10.1002/ev

André Gide, for example, who had earlier proclaimed strong support for the Russian Revolution and its calls for an end to privilege, went on a visit to Moscow in 1936 to speak at Maxim Gorky's funeral. He returned after 3 months with a totally unexpected indictment of what he had seen. Among other things, he wrote (in his essay entitled "Return from the Soviet Union," 1962) of "infinite poverty," of conspicuous social and economic inequality, and of a disheartening, ongoing governmental equation of dissent with treason. As he noted,

> Culture is directed toward one aim only, the glorification of the Soviet Union; it is not disinterested, and critical discrimination is entirely lacking. Indeed, criticism consists solely in inquiring whether such or such a work is in agreement with the Party line. It is never the Party line which is discussed, but only the question of whether a certain theory tallies with it or not. In the Soviet Union, it is accepted once and for all that on every subject—whatever may be the issue—there can only be one opinion, the right one. And each morning, Pravda tells the people what they need to know, and must believe and think. (Gide, 1962, pp. 287–301)

For his pains, Gide had been denounced by the French Communist press (*L'Humanité* and *Les Lettres Françaises*) and actually shunned by left-leaning scholars and many of his former friends and associates. In short, he became a "non-person" (Lottman, 1982, p. 116). His name disappeared from publications and from the boards of organizations. One of his friends "had to see Gide secretly, for he felt he was being followed by his Communist comrades, who considered it a crime to associate with Gide" (Lottman, 1982, p. 117). And of course this kind of punishment was also intended as a deterrent to other potential dissenters: For example, the novelist Nathalie Sarraute told of having been afraid to talk about how in 1937 she herself had observed police in Moscow,

> [They were] rounding up and shooting people, or shipping them back to camps. I was horrified; still, I didn't breathe a word. They had ostracized the great Gide, and I was just a little fish in the pond. What would have happened to me if I had talked?" (quoted by Karnow, 1997, p. 251).

A world war had come and gone, Gide would die in 1951; his judgment had been discounted, and in Paris people believed individual liberty in the Soviet Union to be flourishing. I myself had known before coming to France that Prokofiev, Shostakovich, and Khachaturian, whose works I played in concert, had been harshly criticized by the Soviet Central Committee secretary, Andrei Zhdanov, for "absorbing modernist creative techniques to the detriment of the listening public, and for shunning accessible Russian folk traditions in favor of inaccessible abstraction" (Morrison, 2009, p. 297). Indeed, they were presented as "emblems of decadent distortion," representing "the contemporary modernist bourgeois culture of Europe and America" and "its complete negation of musical art" (p. 297). Although I had, of course, gone to France to study music and didn't yet worry too much about politics, interference with a composer's right to decide what kind of music he would or would not create hardly seemed like flourishing individual liberty to me. Yet living in Paris, it was impossible to avoid noticing how public opinion was lurching massively toward acceptance of the idea that nowhere in the world was there such justice, freedom of dissent, and equality of condition as in the Soviet Union.

Sartre was very important in the development of this public opinion. In the days when I was living there and, of course, for at least a century before that, people in France expected their writers, artists, philosophers, and other intellectuals to frame the political issues of the day for them (Victor Hugo, for example, with Napoleon III's coup d'état, or Émile Zola with the Dreyfus affair). So it was no surprise that Sartre would take a stand; rather, it was the stand itself that was surprising. After having been an extraordinary defender of liberty in his books and during the German occupation of France, and after having taken thoughtful, humanist positions during the purge of French collaborators that had occurred directly after the war, he suddenly became a down-the-line champion of Soviet politics and propaganda, alleging in 1952 that "the freedom to criticize is total in the USSR" (Lilla, 1998, p. 36) and actually dismissing reports of the existence of concentration camps.

Nonetheless, it was becoming clear that these concentration camps, these gulags, did exist. A Russian diplomat named Victor Kravchenko had written a book about them in 1946, and in 1949 a French version had been published, but it was immediately savaged in Les Lettres Françaises as a "CIA fabrication" (Karnow, 1997, p. 251). Kravchenko then filed a criminal libel suit against the newspaper and won his case in the French courts. Similarly, at the end of 1949 David Rousset, a Parisian editor, published an article on the gulag system, with testimony by Soviet citizens, and called for "an investigatory commission on the Soviet camps" (Lottman, 1982, p. 273). This was again met by rhetorical ferocity in Les Lettres Françaises, accusing Rousset of falsifying documents. Rousset, like Kravchenko, then sued for criminal libel, and he also won damages. In a joint letter to The New York Times, Arthur Koestler, Reinhold Niebuhr, Arthur Schlesinger, and others wrote of this French trial that it had been "nothing less than a full-dress indictment of the entire system of slave labor in the Soviet Union" (Lottman, 1982, pp. 273–274).

None of these events, however, appeared to penetrate public opinion in Paris, and I could see almost no change in the attitudes expressed by the artists, writers, musicians, critics, and other intellectuals I knew. The one notable exception came in the case of Albert Camus, who had been slowly veering away from Sartrean positions on human rights in the Soviet Union. In 1951, he published a book called The Rebel, in which he expressed his view that the Stalinist system had to be fought and that Soviet prison camps were a fundamental problem.

Camus believed that when a revolution was not serving its aims, its failure must be pointed out, but at the end of the 1940s, progressive French intellectuals chose to ignore Communist police-state abuses and gulags in order not to imperil the revolution in general. ... Camus saw that the USSR was a land of slaves and yet, as he noted, "its concentration-camp rule is adored as an instrument of liberation and a school for future happiness." (Todd, 1997, p. 301)

This book was, of course, badly received by Sartre and his associates. Sartre split with Camus publicly in 1952, "practicing excommunication with even more verve than the pope of surrealism, André Breton, had ever done" (Todd, 1997, p. 308). Sartre's magazine, *Les Temps Modernes,* reviewed *The Rebel* harshly, Camus responded, then Sartre, and the dispute went on and on. Although the venom of this unrestrained venting was widely discussed, public opinion itself still seemed largely unaffected: The idea of the Soviet Union as "the unsurpassable horizon of our time" (Lilla, 1998, p. 36) seemed to have taken root permanently. To me, it was unspeakably depressing to see Camus become a nonperson like Gide before him, and for the same reason. Raymond Aron, again reviewing *The Rebel*, would later write:

> Camus not only objected to certain aspects of Soviet reality, but he also saw the Communist regime as total tyranny which had been inspired and justified by a philosophy. ... Camus reproached revolutionaries for sacrificing living people to a supposed historical good, a historical good whose exact image was contradictory, and in any case, incompatible with existentialism. (Todd, 1997, pp. 308–310)

Eventually, in 1956 Krushchev made his famous speech against the evils of Stalinism, but it wasn't widely reported until much later, and even then his words were taken in Paris as the fulminations of a rival political leader: Nothing much changed in public opinion. But finally 6 years later in 1962, something happened. A French translation of Aleksandr Solzhenitsyn's book *One Day in the Life of Ivan Denisovich* was published, and the whole carefully constructed Sartrean networking edifice fell apart. Yet this book was not at all histrionic: Its drama was understated, it had no perceptible agenda; it simply portrayed the conditions of existence, from reveille to sunset, of a man sentenced to a Siberian prison camp.

But in a Parisian world that still had not grasped the impossibility of dissent or the presence of gulags in the Soviet Union, the publication of this book marked the beginning of the disintegration of these and other myths. I'm not suggesting that the work was not wonderfully written; it was. But the power of the book lay, it seemed to me, in the fairly stolid presentation of an unmistakably recognizable reality (i.e., the experiences of a

Russian peasant who doesn't complain but accepts every unjustifiable thing that comes his way) and in the modest, quiet manner in which Solzhenitsyn deploys his data, with readers seeing everything through Ivan's eyes (Solzhenitsyn, 1962).

This work had a truly extraordinary effect, bringing down not only mistaken beliefs, but also the people who believed them, and even the role that public intellectuals had played in the political life of France. As Mark Lilla (1998) commented,

> [T]he days when intellectuals turned to philosophers to get their political bearings, and the public turned to intellectuals are all but over. The figure of the "philosophe engagé" promoted by Sartre has been badly tarnished by the political experiences of the past several decades, beginning with the publication of Solzhenitsyn's books. (p. 40)

How did this happen? Why is it that Solzhenitsyn was not also successfully savaged and banished in Paris, as Gide, Kravchenko, Rousset, and Camus had been before him? First, I think, because of the quality and modesty of the writing, as well as the sense of authenticity that emerged from the book. But also time had passed, it was getting harder to suppress demonstrable facts about "alleged" gulags, and Solzhenitsyn, this unknown professor of mathematics from Ryazan who had himself spent 8 years in a Soviet gulag, was simply too credible a witness. Indeed, the world of Paris changed in 1962 because of this book.

I carried away two ideas from these events that I later used in my evaluation work: (a) the value of networking as a means to credibility, and (b) the power of a credible dissenting voice to disrupt that networking.

The Use of Networking as a Component of Credibility

Simone de Beauvoir's autobiography gives a good account of the networking mechanisms used by Sartre and the French political left to affect public opinion (de Beauvoir, 1992, pp. 230–262). These included weekly meetings, peaceful demonstrations, articles in newspapers and magazines, use of intimidation (as well as shaming and shunning) for dissenters, and the energetic mobilization of intellectual elites. All of these mechanisms taken together—and de Beauvoir offers an amazing number of examples, from simple to complex, from costless to very expensive, for exerting pressure on public opinion—had been quite staggeringly successful for over a decade, as I had seen in Paris. So when I started work at NATO and grasped the weakness of evaluation in a world of politics, I immediately began trying to develop a network of analysts within the International Staff division.

Later, at MITRE Corporation (a U.S. think tank), both of my symposia (one on the use of evaluation in the federal government and another on its institutionalization at state and local levels) were efforts to enlarge and strengthen evaluation networks. Then in 1980, when I went to the Government Accountability Organization (GAO) and experienced the effectiveness and sophistication of special interest groups and others in directly obstructing the use of evaluation findings, I began to think about building a considerably expanded network to strengthen the credibility of our own evaluation work.

Obviously, my goals were not at all the same as those of the Sartrean organization: As evaluators we were not selling anything to anybody or trying to influence public opinion; on the contrary, nonpartisanship and nonadvocacy were hallmarks of our effort. We wanted only to strengthen our credibility to ensure that our findings would be fairly and carefully considered by sponsors and users in the political environment that surrounds evaluation, something that can be hard to achieve in the face of opposition by groups like medical device manufacturers, the National Rifle Association, or the beer lobby (to mention only those). As a result, although the networking infrastructure that I eventually developed at GAO owed a great deal to the Sartrean model, it emphatically excluded both the excommunication of dissenters and the intimidation of innovation within or outside our organization. Not only are these practices disturbing in themselves, they run counter to the building of a strong evaluation process, which needs both dissent and innovation. In any case, as evaluators we were in the business of telling the truth, not of persuading people to implement some larger theoretical/philosophical principle or goal.

So I decided to concentrate first on an advisory board with carefully selected representatives from academia, government, industry, science and technology, and media, whose professional perspectives went from engineering, political science, economics, sociology, psychology, statistics, anthropology, budgeting and policy analysis, through all of the subject areas I knew we would need to study. I also set up a program for visiting scholars to allow expert criticism of our ongoing work, and I instituted relationships with various university social science departments. Additionally, I tried to develop new mechanisms of dissemination, including publication of articles on evaluation (especially evaluation methods), and I pushed international attention to evaluation in a variety of different arenas. To encourage dissent within our office, I set up monthly meetings specifically for staff to bring up evaluative or workplace problems and issues for debate, to make us aware of new ideas in their various fields and to propose better ways of planning, organizing, and implementing upcoming studies.

However, for me the afflicting situation of the nonperson in Paris had been a cautionary tale—especially the fate of Camus, whom I knew personally, dying in 1960 before he could see the effects of Solzhenitsyn's book. And it was also a painful lesson in the importance of limits, of boundaries, on the strategy and tactics of networking that must be placed on any effort to use it for bolstering credibility, no matter how noble or reasonable the goals of that effort.

The Power of a Single Authentic Voice

The Solzhenitsyn example was an enduring source of courage to me in pursuing the results of some accountability evaluations. Although there have been many instances in the past of working scientists or philosophers expressing unpopular views that were eventually vindicated, this single voice was especially impressive, not just because of its singularity, but because of the size and power of the public opinion juggernaut it had destroyed. Just remembering the effectiveness of this one book in the face of hardened conventional wisdom gave me a persistence that I might never have had without seeing its successful disruption of myths in Paris. I thought of it frequently, especially during my 9 years of evaluating the chemical warfare program of the Department of Defense, and I believe that it still carries an important lesson of courage and hope for evaluators.

It's a fact of life that we often lose the struggle to get our findings considered seriously and used in policy making. But I think it helps to remember that speaking out obstinately is sometimes necessary in negotiations in a political environment, and that with time and patience, even a small voice if it's credible has a good chance to be heard. Evaluators, like artists, are, in Seamus Heaney's words, "on the side of undeceiving the world" (Fox, 2013, p. B14), and what I think that means is being vigilant and skeptical but also hopeful in the public realm. As Heaney wrote,

> History says, Don't hope
> On this side of the grave.
> But then, once in a lifetime
> The longed-for tidal wave
> Of justice can rise up
> And hope and history rhyme. (Fox, 2013, p. B14)

References

de Beauvoir, Simone (1992). *Force of circumstance: The autobiography of Simone de Beauvoir* (1st Paragon House ed.). New York: Paragon House.

Fox, M. (2013, August 31). On Seamus Heaney (1939–2013): He wove Irish strife and soil into silken verse. *New York Times*, p. B14.

Gide, A. (1962). Return from the Soviet Union. In H. Guth (Ed.), *Essays* (pp. 287–301). Belmont, CA: Wadsworth Publishing Company.

Karnow, S. (1997). *Paris in the fifties*. New York: Random House.

Lilla, M. (1998, June 25). The politics of Jacques Derrida. *The New York Review of Books*, pp. 36–41.

Lottman, H. R. (1982). *The Left Bank*. Boston, MA: Houghton Mifflin.

Morrison, S. (2009). *The people's artist: Prokofiev's Soviet years*. New York, NY: Oxford University Press.

Solzhenitsyn, A. (1962). *One day in the life of Ivan Denisovich*. New York, NY: Signet Books.

Todd, O. (1997). *Albert Camus: A life*. New York, NY: Alfred A. Knopf, Inc.

ELEANOR CHELIMSKY is a consultant for evaluation policy and methodology, was a Fulbright scholar in Paris, an economic and statistical analyst at NATO, president of both the Evaluation Research Society and the American Evaluation Association, and director for 14 years of the Program Evaluation and Methodology Division at the GAO.

NEW DIRECTIONS FOR EVALUATION • DOI: 10.1002/ev

House, E. (2016). Childhood influences on my work. In D. D. Williams (Ed.), *Seven North American evaluation pioneers*. *New Directions for Evaluation, 150*, 65–68.

6

Childhood Influences on My Work

Ernie House

Abstract

House tells stories about his childhood experiences with adults who were making what he felt were poor evaluations. He had similar evaluation experiences as a teacher and slowly developed his own views about how evaluation could be most fairly and appropriately accomplished in everyday life. He began applying these ideas and many others when he was put in charge of a national evaluation in the 1960s, drawing upon perspectives of many colleagues he assembled to give him advice. He retained a healthy skepticism that typifies all his work, based on the childhood convictions he developed through observing and defending himself from poor adult evaluations. © 2016 Wiley Periodicals, Inc., and the American Evaluation Association.

Experiences in Evaluation

In the first grade our teacher put a chart on the wall with our names on it. She said, in her best grade school teacher voice, "Children, if you do this, you will get a blue star; if you do that, you get a silver star; and if you do this, you get a gold star!" I thought, *she doesn't think we're going to fall for that, does she?* To my astonishment, the other kids began falling all over themselves to win these stars. I felt like yelling, "You idiots, they're just little paper stars!" (Perhaps a portent of evaluations yet to come.)

By that time I was living with my mother, who was working three shifts in a munitions factory while my grandmother took care of my sister and me.

My father had been killed in a car wreck 2 years earlier. My mother had no other means of support and no resources. After a few years she married a man from the factory she didn't know very well, and we moved along a lonely rural highway miles out of town. Unfortunately, the guy turned out to be psycho.

At night they would get into violent arguments, and sometimes he would bring out a loaded gun and hold it to my head, hammer cocked. It was a way of threatening her. I don't know if you've had the opportunity to have an experience like this, but it's totally mind focusing. During these episodes my mind was absolutely lucid. I could see that he was deranged, and I sat perfectly still, in complete control of my emotions. No crying, pleading, or moving. I didn't know what might set him off. I did think that if I survived, I would never allow myself to get into such a helpless situation again. From these and other experiences, I developed a strong resolve and motivation not to be controlled by others.

Another conclusion I had reached by the age of eight was that adults made bad decisions that could prove disastrous for them and for my sister and me. My mother was the best person I ever knew, good through and through, actually too good for the world in which she lived. She was in extremely difficult circumstances, doing the best she could. My father and his four brothers were the toughest people I knew, but hardly models of prudence, as police records show. When they were little, they had been sent to a St. Louis orphanage and farmed out as child laborers after their own father died of silicosis working in the mines in southern Illinois. I reasoned that if I could see through adult motivations and anticipate what adults might do, I could protect my sister and myself. At an early age I began looking beneath the surface of people and events, and I looked suspiciously. This attitude evolved into an intellectual style.

Years later these traits became useful in evaluation. Often, I can see what others do not see, and I will say what others will not say. All people practice willful ignorance to a greater or lesser degree. They choose not to see things—a luxury I felt I could not afford. I pushed willful ignorance back further than most people can tolerate. In books, articles, and high-profile evaluations, I employed these skills.

I was pressured in various ways, as you often are. After all, careers, reputations, and livelihoods are at risk. One of the strangest episodes was a review of environmental education in Austria for the Organization for Economic Development and Cooperation (OECD). The Austrians were so upset with my report that they sent a formal diplomatic protest to OECD. Not every evaluator can say that. Of course, I was highly resistant to such pressures. What could they do? Hold a gun to my head?

This style had carry-over to other parts of my life, as in financial investing. To my great surprise, when I began managing my retirement funds, I found investing fascinating. In a way it was a pure form of evaluation that culminated in concrete gains and losses, unlike contemplating the inadequacy of Hume's theory of causation. And I was good at it. Investing requires skills—skills of skepticism similar to those I had developed in evaluation.

In retrospect, I didn't make the same mistakes as the adults of my childhood. No. I made other mistakes instead. Really, you can't see through everything all the time. You can't live without some illusions. You need illusions to motivate and protect you. Decades ago I said that people are able to withstand far less evaluation than they think they can. That includes me.

How did these childhood experiences affect my work? When conducting evaluations, I don't necessarily believe what people tell me. I validate what they say with other data and with what others say. I have a keen sense of looking beyond appearances towards what lies beneath. My motive is to develop a deeper understanding, with the idea of preventing serious mistakes.

I also empathize with the poor and powerless. Evaluators typically come from the same backgrounds as those in charge, whereas those receiving benefits come from the lower social classes or else are children, patients, or victims, helpless to protect themselves. Empathy with the poor and powerless has prompted me to hold strong positions about social justice, which I have tried to incorporate into evaluation.

Used inappropriately, evaluations can be instruments of repression. I've tried to advance standards that evaluators should live by, and have conducted meta-evaluations to show what evaluators should do. I've been partial to qualitative methods that focus on what people actually experience. Often those in charge do not know what's happening, and sometimes they do not want to know. Willful ignorance is widespread.

Of course, no perspective encompasses the entire truth, and the evaluator's task is to make sense of many perspectives using multiple methods. My skepticism applies to people and methods. No method delivers unequivocal truth. I'm skeptical of foundational positions based on methods or ideology. Evaluators need to look at evidence cautiously and holistically.

I have been bold in challenging authorities. If I arrive at a position not favored by those in power, I expect them to pressure me to change my views and to retaliate if I don't. I am willing to change findings if I have missed something or the issue is unimportant. However, if the issue is critical, that's another matter. How seldom those in power encounter principled opposition is indicated by how uncomfortable they are with it. They realize that professionals are vulnerable in their concern about their own careers, and since those in power can help or hinder, they expect professionals to play along.

In summary, characteristics that influence how I approach evaluation include skepticism and resolve, which lead me to maintain an autonomous viewpoint, question authority, look beneath the surface, resist pressure, control emotion, and empathize with the poor and powerless. No doubt, other evaluators share some of these traits, which they've developed from different backgrounds. And although these traits are well suited to evaluating, being too critical, too suspicious, too cynical, or too provocative can be quite counterproductive. I have been guilty of such missteps on many occasions.

ERNIE HOUSE is an emeritus professor of education at the University of Colorado at Boulder.

NEW DIRECTIONS FOR EVALUATION • DOI: 10.1002/ev

Patton, M. Q. (2016). From evangelist to utilization-focused evaluator. In D. D. Williams (Ed.), *Seven North American evaluation pioneers. New Directions for Evaluation, 150*, 69–76.

7

From Evangelist to Utilization-Focused Evaluator

Michael Quinn Patton

Abstract

Patton tells stories about how he became a youth revivalist, a missionary for his church, and then a humanist. He makes connections between these experiences and his utilization-focused approach to evaluation. © 2016 Wiley Periodicals, Inc., and the American Evaluation Association.

Experiences in Evaluation

As I reflect back on my trajectory to evaluation practitioner, I sense some influences that linger. I'll try to make sense of those with the caveat that I'll be giving coherence to a narrative that I experienced more as fortune and opportunity than intentionality.

My parents met when they were both serving in the army during World War II. I was born in 1945 as the war ended. My father was a factory clerk. We lived in Dayton, Ohio where my father had grown up. I grew up as the oldest of four children in a very religious family of Southern Baptists. I spent a great deal of time in church, much of it in Bible study. I did much more intensive study in church than I ever did in school. We parsed verses sentence by sentence and worried about the exact meaning, trying to understand the divine intent of those words.

Religious Immersion

My mother died from a toxemic pregnancy when I was 12, and that was certainly the pivotal event of my youth. As a 12-year-old, I was comforted by the explanation that God had some greater purpose. To find this greater purpose, I became deeply engaged with the church to the point that during my high school years I became a youth fellowship preacher leading Southern Baptist revival campaigns. A weekend revival required four sermons: Friday night, Saturday night, Sunday morning, and Sunday night. In the Friday night sermon I basically relived my mother's death, telling young people forced to come to the revival by their parents that they ought not to take their parents for granted because they could never know what was going to happen. This message began to attract quite large audiences. The remaining sermons reinforced the message that life can change very quickly so young people shouldn't wait to live the way they knew they should be living. I delivered sermons on how married couples ought to live their lives together, pontificating about what an ideal marriage was, and that too attracted crowds to the revival meetings.

As I look back, what I think I was learning was how to target my message to accomplish the desired outcome. And the outcome was very clear and measured: the number of people who came forward at the end of the sermon and made a personal commitment to Jesus as their Lord and Savior. We did counts at the end of every session and kept graphs. I got feedback about which of my sermons yielded the largest number of saved souls. And it was a pay-for-performance system, because I got a cut of the offering. I didn't think of it quite that way at the time, but subsequently I came to realize that that was what it was. I came to understand, as I was working to enhance my performance, that the basic mechanism was guilt. People were responding to being challenged on whether they were living their lives in accordance with the teachings of Jesus. In retrospect, it was an evaluation message. Here's what Jesus teaches. Look at your life. Are you following those teachings? If not, change. In evaluation terms, it's a classic actual-ideal comparison.

Two things came out of that religious experience. First, I learned public speaking, which has served me well as an evaluation trainer and keynote speaker. Second, perhaps ironically, I honed critical thinking skills. Let me explain. The particular form of Southern Baptist teachings that I was exposed to emphasized an individual relationship with God and individual accountability, which meant that although the church advocated a number of rules to guide behavior, each individual was personally responsible to decide how to behave. For example, whether I should take a newspaper route and deliver papers on Sunday was ultimately my personal decision (and I did it) despite the church teaching that one should not work on the Sabbath. Whether I should go to a school dance or go to certain kinds of movies were my personal decisions. The church minister and youth religious leaders didn't give us rules. They offered guidance (don't dance and don't go to movies) but told us to study the Bible and decide what to do for ourselves. That meant a lot of Bible study. Every day I read Bible passages, prayed, and wrote reflections. I developed as a scholar through these Biblical studies.

I became one of the leading evangelical youth leaders in Ohio. I worked in the Billy Graham evangelical campaign and saw the inner workings of that campaign, which gave rise to doubts as I saw the manipulation of people going on behind the scenes. When I entered college at the University of Cincinnati, I continued to be active in a campus religious fellowship. There was an opportunity for Baptist student leaders to serve as summer missionaries. Between my freshman and sophomore years I served as a youth missionary in the northern part of Peru, near the Ecuador border. I lived with a missionary family, preaching through translation and working with young people there.

That experience in Peru was life changing. Having been preaching for several years about what constituted an ideal marriage, I discovered that the marriages of missionary couples were far from ideal. In my innocence and naiveté, I became disillusioned. I observed the difference between the public persona of these religious role models and their actual behind-the-scenes lives. I got an up-close-and-personal view of people I idealized, and I found out they were petty, bickering, and selfish, often putting their own agendas ahead of what seemed to me the teachings of Christ. I was young and idealistic, and it was a shock to me to see these devout Christians doing some very un-Christian things.

But the most jarring part of the experience in Peru was working in inner city barrios, among the poorest of the poor. I came to know people who were living perfectly monogamous and wholesome lives, at least as far as I knew, but because they didn't have birth certificates, were not legally married, and couldn't afford the 25 dollars to get a birth certificate and a marriage license, they could not be baptized and were therefore condemned to spend eternity in hell. To think that good, decent people were going to spend eternity in hell because they were too poor to get legally married struck me as outrageous and unjust. My faith was shaken.

Because I had been reared to believe that either every word in the Bible was literally true or the Bible was not true, my transition from believer to nonbeliever was very quick that summer. I came back from Peru as a nonbeliever. I had begun during my freshman year to be exposed to some social science courses. Having experienced introductory sociology and anthropology courses on how varied cultural beliefs are socially constructed, I was led by the whole missionary experience to question what I had been taught in church: that the Southern Baptist religion is the one true path, the only way to heaven, and that Christ is the answer to everything.

At the end of the summer in Peru, there was a big convention of all the student missionaries in Laureate, New Mexico. For three days, I spent each evening in the mountains looking for signs from God. For me it became an all-or-nothing proposition. Either Christianity was the one true religion and the Bible was literally true, which was how I was raised, or it was all a sham. I could not bring myself to start picking and choosing which parts of the Bible I was going to believe. It was either the inspired word of God with every word literally true, or it was just another book written by ordinary men and Christianity was just one of many socially constructed religions. When I returned to campus for my sophomore year, I had completely lost my faith; I became an atheist and have been an atheist since that time.

But because of the way the trip to Peru was financed, when I returned as a nonbeliever I still had an obligation to do a year of preaching, and I felt that I needed to meet that obligation. Actually, that year I did the best preaching I ever did, and it foreshadowed the "preaching" I still do as an evaluator. Basically my sermon became like this:

> This is what the Bible says, and this is what Jesus says. Either it's true or it's not true. If it's true, look at your life, evaluate how you're living your life, and change if you're not following Christ's teachings. If, on the other hand, the Bible is not true, then stop pretending that you believe. But if you examine your life, you'll probably find that you are not living your life in accordance with scripture. Look at what the Bible says about striving for and accumulating material wealth. Look at what it says about how you treat people. Look at what it says about war.

It seems to me in retrospect that I had happened upon and crafted an evaluation message: "This is what the Bible says about how to live. Compare how you are living to those criteria and judge how well you're doing. If you're not living that way, then either change or stop calling yourself a Christian." I never said anything about my own doubts and loss of faith. My way of making peace with the obligation to continue preaching was to focus on the Bible's teachings not my own beliefs. It was a disingenuous and convoluted compromise, replete with mental gymnastics and cognitive dissonance, and when I had fulfilled my post-Peru 3-month obligation, I was never seen at the youth fellowship again.

What I think emerged from those experiences and endures to this day was a commitment to reality testing. Get real. Compare what you profess to believe with how you actually behave. What's true and not true? What's working and not working? And how does one know?

The Turn to Social Science

I went to the University in Cincinnati because of its highly regarded engineering program. The first year was filled with required math and science courses, with one humanities requirement—an introductory writing course. We had to write weekly essays about some current affairs topic.

At the time I lived in a boarding house owned by a German landlady. On Sunday nights she would let us watch television with her. One Sunday night, procrastinating because I couldn't think of anything to write about, I went down to watch television with her. It was the night that the Beatles first appeared on the Ed Sullivan variety entertainment show. I was absolutely fascinated watching the effects of the Beatles on young women in the audience who were screaming, going crazy, swooning, and some even passing out. So I wrote my essay about that. The writing professor wrote in the margin of my paper, "If this kind of thing interests you, there are people who study this. You might want to take a sociology class."

So I did—and got hooked. I left engineering, changed my major to sociology, and wrote my senior sociology thesis comparing the popular cultures of the 1940s, 1950s and 1960s as revealed by the music and lyrics of Frank Sinatra, Elvis Presley, and the Beatles.

Cross-Cultural Immersion

I got married right out of college so we could go into the Peace Corps together, because you couldn't go in together if you weren't married. And I was avoiding getting drafted into the Vietnam War. We served as Peace Corps volunteers in eastern Burkina Faso. My wife was assigned to public health support in a clinic for pregnant women. I was in agricultural extension. We lived among the Gourma people, working in very poor rural villages where farmers engaged in subsistence agriculture, growing primarily millet and sorghum. Soils were poor. Water was scarce. Infant mortality was high. Infectious diseases were common and debilitating. Markets were underdeveloped. Resources were few. We were young, idealistic, hopeful, and clueless.

We began by talking with villagers, listening to their stories, gathering their histories, learning about their experiences, and working to understand their perspectives. Gradually, as we learned the language, engaged with the people, and began to understand the local setting, project possibilities emerged: digging wells, building one-room schools, introducing cash crops, experimenting with new approaches to cultivation, organizing cooperatives, and initiating education efforts. But our role was always more one of facilitation than actual doing. We figured out shared interests, helped organize groups for action, and helped people find resources. Our efforts were highly pragmatic, just trying to find something that would work, that might create a little leverage that could be used to gather insights into and start to address larger problems. In the grand scheme of things, our efforts were very modest.

I learned how to figure out what someone cared about, how to bring people together to identify shared interests, and how to match initiatives and resources to those shared interests. I learned to ground my change efforts in the perspectives, values, and interests of those with whom I worked—the indigenous people who were there before I came and would be there after I left. I learned to appreciate and honor local villagers and farmers as the primary stakeholders in change and to see my role as facilitating their actions, not letting my interests and values drive the process, but rather deferring to and facilitating their interests and values. In that way, I tried to make myself useful to people struggling to survive in a harsh environment. My approach to evaluation grew out of those seminal community development experiences in Africa.

From Sociology to Evaluation

After Peace Corps, I got a doctorate in sociology at the University of Wisconsin. When I finished grad school, I had the opportunity to go to the University of Minnesota in one of the first training programs in evaluation. My first son was born at that time when I was teaching a course in introductory sociology. I taught the class with him in a backpack, and a photo of us made the front page of the National Enquirer. I got letters from all over the country, most of them warning about the abuse of subjecting an infant to sociological lectures at an early age and threatening to turn me in to authorities if I continued this abusive practice. I remember being fascinated with these strong emotional reactions and intrigued by the very different ways that people make sense of the world. I had seen the ways that deeply religious people make sense of the world. I had observed how the Gourma people in Burkina Faso made sense of the world. When I happened to have this National Enquirer experience, it deepened my interest in the vastly different perspectives that people bring to whatever they experience and the values that inform our interpretations of our experiences.

A part of what has undergirded my evaluation career has been this continued fascination with different perspectives that people bring to whatever is going on in a program—both those who run programs and those who experience them. An ongoing emphasis in my evaluation practice carries forward from those Baptist revival experiences of inviting people to look at what they believe, look at what they're doing, look at the disparate nature of what they're doing compared to what they believe, and do reality testing about whether they're doing the things they believe and whether they're accomplishing the things that they want to accomplish. That reality testing theme intersects with my interest in multiple perspectives, both of which derive from the early life experiences I've described here.

Personal Problems and Public Issues

Sociology highlights the intersection between individual personal problems and public issues that are the aggregate impact of many individual problems. I've lived that intersection. My youngest brother was born when my mother died. He was 12 years younger than I was. My father wasn't able to take care of him, so he got moved around to different families at church for the first 3 years of his life, which we now understand means that he never experienced the nurturing of deep attachment bonding. He came back to live with us at age three. After I'd left home, was married, and had come back from the Peace Corps, I learned that he was having huge problems in high school. My father's solution was going to be to put him into military school, which I thought would be disastrous. So I took custody of him, and I put him into an alternative school in Minneapolis.

In that program, which was very supportive of troubled young people, he came to recognize himself as gay. He also began dealing with some of the trauma of his childhood. It turned out he'd been having very dangerous, promiscuous, at-risk homosexual encounters in bus stations in Dayton, Ohio from the time he was 10 years old. He had been preyed on by boys in the neighborhood and by men in public parks. He entered a long-term supportive relationship after high school, but subsequently contracted AIDS and died in the early days of the epidemic before there were any drug therapies available. The experience of trying to work with him and get him help gave me direct experience with a number of social services and contacts with people in the helping professions.

I got to see up close how challenging it is to work with people as troubled as my brother was. Many tried to help him, but the barriers were immense. What I observed and learned through the travails of my brother often comes up as I work with human service providers, letting them know I understand the challenges they face. For example, my brother lived on the streets for a period, and my credibility in working with agencies serving homeless youth is enhanced knowing that I've had direct experience with the challenges they face.

Reflective Practice as a Parent

I wrote a book about taking my oldest son into the Grand Canyon for a coming of age (initiation) experience (Patton, 1999). A lot of that book is my effort to think about the experience of parenting and looking at what it means to be a good father. How would one know? That book looks at some of the experiences reported here and how they influenced my approach to parenting. As my three children became young adults, the central message of parenting was that they had to make their own decisions, as I had learned that I had to make my own decisions, and that a part of being able to make decisions is to be adept at weighing consequences, which basically is evaluative thinking. I would say to them, "Every action has consequences, so examine the potential consequences of your actions. Look at how things are unfolding as they unfold. If what you're doing isn't working, change what you're doing." All three of my children have been through my evaluation workshops, so they know—and laugh about—the overlap of my messages as a father and my reality-testing messages as an evaluator.

From Faith Based to Evidence Based

In 2001, when President George H. Bush began his faith-based initiatives, I was giving a keynote address at a national convention of human service providers about evaluation use. At the end of my speech, the first question was whether evaluators knew anything about evaluating faith-based initiatives? I thought for a moment and said, "Well, from an evaluation perspective, all initiatives are faith based until they've been evaluated." That question put me in touch with the way in which my experience of religious faith in my youth has shaped my journey into evaluation. My response reflects how I make sense of those experiences.

Reference

Patton, M. Q. (1999). *Grand Canyon celebration: A father–son journey of discovery.* New York: Prometheus Books.

MICHAEL QUINN PATTON *is an independent organizational development and program evaluation consultant and a former president of the American Evaluation Association.*

NEW DIRECTIONS FOR EVALUATION • DOI: 10.1002/ev

Kushner, S. (2016). Autobiography as case study. In D. D. Williams (Ed.), *Seven North American evaluation pioneers. New Directions for Evaluation, 150*, 77–83.

8

Autobiography as Case Study

Saville Kushner

Abstract

Kushner comments on the rest of this issue and offers suggestions for future work and the future of evaluation. © 2016 Wiley Periodicals, Inc., and the American Evaluation Association.

Gary Werskey, in *The Visible College*, wrote what he called a *collective biography* (Werskey, 1988). His study of five high-ranking Cambridge scientists was written to illuminate the seamless connections between experience, science, and politics. His subjects were well chosen—all members of an academic and social elite and all committed to radical socialism. Though prominent as individuals, each with his own unique story to tell; as a group (a "visible college") they cohered around a narrative of disenchantment and hope, of imperial collapse and redemption through the purity of science, of privilege, and of obligation. Their science was the countervailing historical force to the failings of capitalism. Scientific advancement—both in career and in theoretical insight—was a case of moral gain: "making professional advancement as much into a political duty as a personal aspiration" (Publisher's foreword). This was a phenomenon of the interwar years in Britain—an ideological "enlightenment" in science.

There we start and end the comparison with evaluation. Take out the elitism, the privilege, and the socialism (the guts of Werskey's story), and we have some insight into what is happening in this tiny niche of public theorizing that is this NDE issue. Here we have a "collective autobiography" of some of those who were the high scientists of program and policy evaluation, a collective entering into an ethical practice, an expression of social valuing. These are personal stories of redemption and change, but the accounts of personal transformation conceal a subtext of wider social and political change. The period marked by the childhood and growth of our authors was the post-Depression era (when Werskey's scientists were active and influential), where modern(istic) governments learned the utility of organized social experimentation to drive social change, giving to the new science of experimental sociology the "laboratories" they needed (Oakley, 1998). Here is an emergent "enlightenment" narrative.

We may learn about these individuals, we may not (there is, for example, no ideological thread here), but through their speculations and reflections we might somehow construct a narrative of this unusual practice that is contemporary evaluation—or rather a narrative of its development in those turbulent but expansive years of the 1960s and the 1970s. This was the basis of my own encouragement to David Williams to publish these stories, a "walking backwards into the future." If we do not encounter "new directions" in these accounts, we will certainly encounter the experience of taking a new direction. In these days of rampant Taylorism in universities— part of Zygmunt Bauman's (2012) "liquefaction" of intellectual structures— the challenge of discovering a new generation of radical and innovative theorists seems to intensify:

> To cut a long story short: if in its "solid" phase the heart of modernity was in controlling and fixing the future, in the "liquid" phase the prime concern moved to ensuring the future was not mortgaged, and to averting the threat of any pre-emptive exploitation of the still undisclosed, unknown and unknowable opportunities the future was hoped to and was bound to bring. (Bauman, Foreword to the 2012 Edition)

In the urgency to "liquidize" we "liquidate." To make doctoral enquiry more Taylor-efficient, we dismantle those conservative structures that have served to sustain academic independence and student autonomy. We train and ethically regulate our research students and insist upon their reading the canon prior to engaging with research—we even induct them into our preferred methodologies. As we do, we risk crowding out of university exchange that methodological creativity and spirit of independence that fosters innovation and deliciously uncertain futures, which characterized the induction of our authors. Liquidity seems paradoxically to disable more than enable future generations.

If I may recount an anecdote—at the Centre for Applied Research in Education (University of East Anglia, United Kingdom) we once gave a PhD scholarship to a bright English Literature graduate named Richard

Davies. We wanted to develop the writing strand of our research and evaluation program. Barry MacDonald issued an instruction to the Centre: No one was to talk methodology to Richard, and he was asked not to read methodological texts. He was, nonetheless, part of an impassioned community of methodologists. Richard was sent into a youth prison to conduct research free of guidelines or training—institutional review boards had not yet been inflicted on the university. He started his thesis with an observation (which I recall and loosely paraphrase): *I am sitting in a room, facing me a young offender. There is nothing but a table with a melamine top, two chairs and a panic button on the wall. He has a striped shirt, jeans and nothing else. I have a jacket, a notebook, a pen, a wedding ring and a purpose. We are unequal. What am I supposed to do?* Richard ended up writing at a leading edge of methodology—writing as method (Davies, 1986).

It is in the intensifying absence of such possibilities that this NDE issue is laden with importance. The democratic space for public and evaluative critique and personal exploration is diminishing. In his Foreword to *The Visible College*, Robert Young, the publisher, gives a primary reason "why I am reprinting this book": "the future—indeed, the very existence—of civilisation depends on getting right the relationship between expertise and democracy." Much of evaluation is implicitly concerned with this challenge, some of it explicitly so. We might even say that much evaluation, both theory and practice, treats it as a substantive concern, as do a number of these writers. In evaluation more than in the natural sciences, each action and interaction raises questions of the right to know, the obligation to inform public knowledge, participation of citizens, the accountabilities of the observer, and the public validity of claims. Gibbons (1999) analyzed the shift from *reliable science* (replicable, probative) to *socially robust science* (publicly negotiated, plausible), and evaluation has been one of the disciplines that ran at the vanguard of the pack. Methodologies and principles were developed with this precisely in mind, some from our authors. These stories cover just that moment in modern history when the shift was being made.

We need to reflect again on what it takes to be a methodological innovator, because that particular torch needs to be passed on as we invite a new generation into that same preoccupation with expertise and democracy. I hope this collective autobiography finds its way into the hands of research supervisors. But the evaluation doctorate suggests another balance to be struck: that between socially robust evaluative enquiry and the doctorate as a personal journey. Though Werskey's account is of an intellectual movement, it is made up of the personal preferences and insights of five self-determining individuals. Evaluation invites self-determination too, as we face a range of methodological choices that invite self-expression and emotional leaning. There is a great deal of emotion in these autobiographies—surely a model for authority-oppressed research students. What stories will they tell?

So What Do We Have Here, and What Do We Not Have?

First, we have a collection of North American evaluation thinkers—all part of a post-Tylerian movement. This is significant in that it plays to a tendency toward academic *exceptionalism* in the United States that has sometimes overlooked the real richness of exchange between Europe, Australasia and the United States, and has cited too little the work of creative evaluation thinkers who were in at the beginnings of the discipline (I do not have myself in mind, but my mentors). David's interview program bucks the trend and covers many of them, though they are not here represented. This is significant in representing the contemporary roots of evaluation, for there were circumstances unique to the United Kingdom and Spain, for example, but which paralleled the Kennedy/Johnson context in stimulating the demand for such a discipline and practice (Norris, 1990). For example, the work of the Universities of Málaga and Valladolid in pioneering program evaluation was a purposeful response to the fall of the Franco fascist dictatorship. Evaluation in the United Kingdom was almost exclusively fueled in its early years by a curriculum-/school-reform movement with free interchange of ethical and political principles between curriculum and evaluation discourses (Kushner, 2009). This takes nothing away from this selection; it is, if anything, a sin of omission not of commission. But watch out for further publications from David.

Much autobiography wobbles precariously along a line separating self-denial, self-regard, and self-deception. Bud Peshkin (1988) famously wrote of his six "subjectivities" lying in the "subjective underbrush of the research experience"—from the "Ethnic Maintenance I" to the "Pedagogical-Meliorist I." It has sometimes been said, bemusedly but sympathetically, that the more authentic "I" was the seventh. Peshkin talks in a postmodern way about "situation subjectivities," and this is perhaps a good way to characterize these accounts. Some are more perfunctory than others: some written with a relish for the task, others perhaps with a different predisposition. But they all appeal to individual circumstances to which the authors had to respond as individuals.

The subjectivities revealed in this text are those of harsh or tender childhood moments, of being in the presence of geopolitical shifts, or of ideas carefully constructed around an extended metaphor. It is commonplace to observe that there would be perhaps five other subjectivities available in each case, and we may take a little skeptically that these recounted moments were as definitive and deterministic as they are sometimes portrayed.

Nonetheless, those portrayed here have to be heard. These were some of the innovators of our important discipline, and innovations demand to be understood through their actors and the dramas they are bound up in (MacDonald, 1976). More important, these were people who were courageous, creative, and privileged to have provoked a Kuhnian upheaval in their discipline. This surely makes for rehearsed reflection and a resolution of self-doubt that others can learn from—more so than in the rest of us who toil at more humdrum labors of following opportunities and pathways laid out by our intellectual leaders. These are people who at some stage of their career brought to the forefront of their thinking a theorizing over values, careers, movements.

What we do not have here is the extensive interview-based theorizing over a life, or indeed over multiple lives. I do not refer to the application of a sociological or a psychological theory, but to evidence of second-order thinking provoked by a reflective interview, perhaps the grounding for generating a theory of methodological innovation. We have a sense of raw data, unaffected by challenge or speculation. We are in the business of evaluation, and a common trope is that evaluation process and method should reflect the nature of the field under study. What then makes for an evaluative interview of an evaluator? All of those represented here are accomplished critical enquirers—what would we expect of a skilled self-interview (what Rob Walker once called an "intraview")?

Perhaps we should also ask how the responsibility for understanding/theorizing about contingency gets shared between evaluand and audience. The reader is dissatisfied when one of our authors fails to explain the connections between his or her experience and evaluation practice, and yet we are equally dissatisfied when the explanation is made.

One is too relativistic, the other too reductionist. Of course, there are insufficient data to engage in robust theorizing: we hear almost nothing of the remarkable accomplishment of shifting personal paradigm—of the switch from psychological modeling to evaluative and political theorizing, for example. But this too gives insight into the challenge of evaluation engaging its audiences as active agents. It reminds us of the choice we face between stimulating or displacing the judgment of authors. In a loose sense, what this issue of NDE provides is a case study in methodological innovation, just as Werskey's account is a single case study of the politics of science. How do we arrive at the case study?

The conventional answer would be that we generalize from an instance—or in this case generalize from an instance to a broader context and then back to the instance. Let me explain. We learn something from these accounts about the emergence from early (often childhood) experience of commitments and predispositions. These are positioned within a broader social/psychological/political context: the Great Depression, flatland culture of the Midwest, schooling, urban poverty, evangelist movements, shifts in intellectual cultures. But occasionally we can work back from those broader contexts to understand better the instance itself. There is a kind of iterative process of generalization going on. The more we know of the instance, the greater the insight into the domain, but then the greater the further insight into the instance. It is in that iteration that we squeeze out understanding of early evaluation emergence.

This is nowhere more transparent than in Eleanor Chelimsky's American-in-Paris account, with the broad sweep from personal experience through music theory and on to geopolitics and intellectual movements. Contexts within action, actions within context—all contingent. Here is autobiography as case study. We do not need to read Eleanor's admiration of Schoenberg as deterministic of her taste for methodological innovation; neither her experience of concert playing as the source of her commitment to audience integration; nor her witnessing the machinations of Sartre as decisive in teaching her the value of validation through networking. These are reminders that we live in a contingent world where a *zeitgeist* is processed cognitively and uncertainly. There is no direct pathway from concert to concerted action—it's more like crazy-paving. But we need to know what is in the cognitive mix. Whether or not Eleanor connects an intellectual tendency toward moral seizure with evaluation's challenge to the power of hegemonic narratives, then we at least can. Eleanor has given us the analytic tools and a theory of contingency to work with.

So can we truly learn from these writings? Is our context not too far from the expansive times in which these pioneers were self-forming? Possibly. Who would lay claim to reinvent evaluation—or if evaluation has had its day, to invent its replacement? Which research student supervisor reading this issue is guiding the next innovative theorist? What conditions would enable that innovator to emerge?

The last great period of British austerity, post-World War II, ended in a cultural explosion. When John Osborne wrote *Look Back in Anger* (1956) and Joe Orton contributed *Saturday Night and Sunday Morning* (1958), all aspects of cultural repression were laid bare—threadbare—and made problematic. In *Look Back in Anger*, a woman says to her procrustean father of her rebellious husband: "You're hurt because everything is changed. Jimmy is hurt because everything is the same." They were aware of their positioning, of living on a cusp—actually a precipice—with social contingencies in flux: ♫ "the times they are a 'changing." Apart from Chelimsky's reflections, we don't have a strong sense of these authors living in this same period of flux. Their worlds were unstable, but not in that fundamental sense of social change, not in that sense that Werskey's scientists had that there were historical truths at stake. But there were.

But nor do we yet have a sense of flux in our own social economies. We do not live in an environment, political or scholastic, that persuades us to take the personal risks associated with innovative thinking characteristic of some of our authors here. The commercialization of the university, the centralization of power in education systems, the internalization of evaluation into the administrative system—all of these make allegiance to official logics the safest and most lucrative option. It sometimes seems that the practice that is evaluation has developed over the past 20 years not by accumulating innovative thoughts, but by shedding thoughts too difficult to sustain. Perhaps we are playing a waiting game—perhaps there are sleepers out there

NEW DIRECTIONS FOR EVALUATION • DOI: 10.1002/ev

ready to be activated at the right moment. If so, they will be the most avid and rewarded readers of these accounts.

References

Bauman, Z. (2012). *Liquid modernity*. London: John Wiley.
Davies, R. (1986). *A remand centre education (Unpublished doctoral dissertation)*. University of East Anglia, UK.
Gibbons, M. (1999). Science's new social contract with society. *Nature, 402*, C81–C84.
Kushner, S. (2009). Rediscovering educational purpose in educational evaluation. In *Encyclopaideia, XIII*(26), 9–28.
MacDonald, B. (1976). The portrayal of persons as evaluation data. Paper presented at the annual conference of the American Educational Research Association, San Francisco, CA. Retrieved from http://www.uea.ac.uk/education/research/care/resources /archive/barry-macdonald
Norris, N. (1990). *Understanding educational evaluation*. London: Kogan Page.
Oakley, A. (1998). Experimentation and social interventions: A forgotten but important history. *British Medical Journal, 317*, 1239–1242.
Peshkin, A. (1988). In search of subjectivity: One's own. *Educational Researcher, 17*, 17–21.
Werskey, G. (1988). *The visible college: A collective biography of British scientists and socialists of the 1930s* (2nd ed.). London: Free Association Books.

SAVILLE KUSHNER is professor of Public Evaluation at the University of Auckland and Chair of the Evaluation and Research Board, New Zealand Aid. He is an advocate for Democratic Evaluation and Case Study.

Williams, D. D. (2016). Connections, themes, and implications for the future of evaluation. In D. D. Williams (Ed.), *Seven North American evaluation pioneers. New Directions for Evaluation, 150*, 85–105.

9

Connections, Themes, and Implications for the Future of Evaluation

David Dwayne Williams

Abstract

This final article explores some of the unique and common connections the seven early and influential evaluators have made between their extraprofessional and professional evaluation lives, as reflected in their comments and stories in their individual articles and one prominent theme noted across all cases: These evaluators described how their values developed and eventually shaped their evaluation approaches. In addition, some subthemes are identified and questions for further study are posed. Following, in one page each, the seven authors review their colleagues' articles and offer their own responses regarding what they learned from each other and what possible implications they foresee for future evaluation. Based on these reviews, readers are invited to think about possible implications for their own and their clients' evaluation lives. The entire document invites readers to relate to evaluation less as a technology and more as a values-based activity involving their own values and those of other participants in their evaluations. © 2016 Wiley Periodicals, Inc., and the American Evaluation Association.

A Prominent Theme: Values and Valuing

Many philosophers, historians, and others have explored relationships between values and valuing through axiology (e.g., Hart & Embree, 1997). Most evaluation theorists have also explored relationships between values and professional evaluation, including notable works by the seven authors included in this issue (e.g., Alkin, Vo, & Christie, 2012; Chelimsky, 2012; House & Howe, 1999; Patton, 2008; Scriven, 2013; Stake, 2004; Stufflebeam, 2001).

But although all these authors have acknowledged that values have major impact on both professional and extraprofessional evaluation, they have offered very little documentation of their own use of values and of connections they make between their values and their extra-professional and professional evaluations. This issue begins to address this gap in the literature. My interviews did not focus exclusively on the authors' values, but as I led them to focus on their particular experiences, interviewees shared stories of their extraprofessional and professional evaluations and offered their own views on how these experiences are or are not connected.

Two questions guided the interviews and analyses of responses from the professional evaluators:

> What have you brought to and built into your influential evaluation practice and theory from your general evaluation life and/or from your more structured formal discipline experience before you became involved with or outside of evaluation as a profession?

> What do you consider to be the implications of your own experience for the field of professional evaluation?

Although they did not explicitly state the position, the common answer apparent in the stories of all of them (articles 1–7) and in the summary provided in Tables 9.1–9.7 was *values*. They brought values they had tested, developed, and used regularly in their extraprofessional evaluation life to their professional evaluation life. Primarily these included values for judging the quality of various aspects of human life as well as values for judging the methods of evaluation people use in daily as well as professional evaluations. And as they have shared their values with others in the field of evaluation, these professional evaluators have built on those values that have paralleled their own and those of their stakeholders.

Connections evaluators make between their own extraprofessional and professional evaluation lives, as summarized in Tables 9.1–9.7, show value connections going back to the stories they shared; this chart uses quotations from their articles (presented in the sequence of their articles). Following the tables, each evaluator's pattern of valuing is summarized briefly, and then themes, questions, and implications are suggested.

Summaries of Authors' Connections

Stake valued his parents' and his pre–evaluation-profession colleagues' divergent values for defining quality and for judging how well evaluands meet

Table 9.1. Robert Stake's connections

Areas of connection	Examples of connections	Manifestation in professional evaluations and views
He noticed values in both parents without thinking they would impact his evaluation life, but drew upon and expanded these values throughout his life and work.	Father was a pharmacist who took great care in ensuring the quality of products he made and sold by using quality ingredients. The idea of caretaking of materials was prominent without Robert Stake being aware that his father was giving him evaluative guidance. His emphasis was that you should look carefully to see who deserves to be given your support or your reward. Mother was a teacher who graded work in terms of the effect her evaluation would have on the student rather than to declare what each student deserved. She said you should carefully look at the effects of the rewards before you decide on how you will give them. The two views did not converge, but they both had an epistemology of rewards to deal with the problems in both their teaching and pharmacy work.	It appears that Stake combined his parents' approaches to evaluation in various ways throughout his life. This is apparent in his 2004 book *Standards-Based and Responsive Evaluation*, in which he seemed to explore his father's perspective when he pushed for standards-based approaches (as he did mostly in his early measurement-oriented career), while he also emphasized a qualitative and responsive approach that in many ways paralleled his mother's views and his own later evaluation career approaches.
Preprofessional evaluation suggests he was exploring his use of conflicting values and criteria.	He wanted evidence, strong measurements and strong grounds for making decisions—with redundancy and with security in the Navy and through a blueprinting and engineering approach to life. But when evaluating to make big decisions such as marriage and choosing graduate school, he appears to have been more subjective and impetuous.	His first formal "countenance" of evaluation paper (1967) and early view of evaluation as measurement echoed criteria demanded by engineering and predictive science, whereas his "responsive" evaluation paper (1973) and later evaluations in his career celebrated the unique, subjective, often-conflicting, and ever-changing values of multiple stakeholders.
Responses to colleagues with conflicting views highlighted his emerging values.	When pursuing a career in psychometrics, he was surprised to find that stakeholders did not respond as he had hoped when he shared his results based on carefully constructed measures. He was persuaded slowly by others who urged studying quality from the stakeholders' perspectives.	He explored evaluating all along the continuum from standards based to responsive, depending on the evaluation situation. His focus on the study of the particular to address stakeholders' values and definitions of quality during his later career contrasts with his focus on psychometric measurement as essentially equivalent to evaluation in his early career.

NEW DIRECTIONS FOR EVALUATION • DOI: 10.1002/ev

Table 9.2. Marvin Alkin's connections

Areas of connection	Examples of connections	Manifestation in professional evaluations and views
His father's example of evaluating demonstrates Marv's early focus on certain values that contrasted with his father's and later recognition of times to respect his father's approach.	"My father … in my mind … made assertions without sufficient evidence to back them up. He was … too nonjudgmental. He saw good in everyone. Even when people took advantage of him, he would say, 'He meant well.' I was a bratty kid who was bothered by his acquiescence and continually argued with him and demanded to know how he could say that—'What's the evidence?' and again, 'How do you know that?'"	"… this search for rational knowledge was the beginning of my evaluation career. My father died at age 59 and I have felt guilty ever since about my 'over the top' rational behavior. Maybe there are times to respect instinct and experience."
Learning to teach and loving to teach are associated with his approach to knowing stakeholders and their values.	"… I enjoy attempting to 'read' students and to determine whether real communication is taking place. Seeking to comprehend where they are coming from and whether they understand the material has been a part of the way that I view teaching."	"I suppose this translates [to my approach] as an evaluator trying to picture stakeholders (potential users) and understand them—to perceive their point of view and the total context."
Valuing the use of simulations and role-play in teaching so students learn by doing relates to his evaluation methods.	"… an important part of my teaching then, as now, involves creating situations in which people can learn by doing—by role-playing … I use scenarios and role-playing as an active part of every class I teach."	"… simulations and playing roles are important parts of the way that I do evaluation. I present scenarios to test whether the primary users' questions really get at what is considered important. Scenarios and role-playing are also a part of the a priori valuing procedure that I use with primary stakeholders."

quality criteria. Eventually, he valued a type of standards-based approach to measurement for some types of evaluations, but he also came to value inviting people to clarify their definitions of quality, while assuming that every definition might be unique. Stake eventually translated these values into his standards-based and responsive approaches to professional evaluation, which have influenced many evaluators throughout the profession.

Alkin valued a mathematical rationality that demanded evidence; he was critical of his father's more instinctual approach to evaluating risks and

Table 9.3. Michael Scriven's connections

Areas of connection	Examples of connections	Manifestation in professional evaluations and views
The constant moving and associated social instability he experienced have a lot to do with his focus on reason.	"… constant shifts meant absolute fracture of all friendships that lasted more than 2 or 3 years. And that meant you either survived without them or you didn't survive, so you survived without them. So that was the start that I think affected my attitude to life to some degree, and eventually my attitude towards the value of reason … "	"… reason … is my main professional area of publication and evaluation."
His mother's choices urged him to take an independent evaluation stand, favoring reason over emotions.	"When I was 14 it became clear to me that my mother's reasoning was no longer operating too well, and so I had to make a decision about whether to stay or go, and I decided to go … I jumped off the train … Boringly, I ran away to school; that is … back to the boys' school I was in, which I thought was a better place."	"… I think that those experiences for me—the choice to go to school, having to run away from home when I was 14—forced a certain amount of independence on me." "… what did become clear was the need to stand with my reasons and not with the affections."
Writing an essay on evaluating acts of valor presaged values and focus of his evaluation career.	"The topic I chose, which is why I found my interest in evaluation is lifelong, was rather peculiar. It was whether one could quantitatively evaluate acts of valor or heroism during the war in the process of awarding medals. That was affected by my orientation towards my father's career and my fixation on being a fighter pilot."	"I won a prize for that essay, which inherited the idea that I was trying to develop mathematics in a way that follows ethics."

judging others. He also loved teaching, which included "reading" students and then using role-plays and simulations to meet them where they were. He combined these values into his approach to evaluating as an administrator and then into his professional evaluations and his writings about evaluation, which have been used by his students and many others

Scriven respected his father as a pilot, and he studied math and science to prepare himself for a similar career. He rejected his mother's religion and "irrational" attempts to move him away from his school because he valued independent thought, rationality, and empirical evidence over what

Table 9.4. Daniel Stufflebeam's connections

Areas of connection	Examples of connections	Manifestation in professional evaluations and views
Close-knit, intact family while experiencing circumstances of poverty due to growing up in the wake of the Great Depression influenced his choice of life-long values.	Strong work ethic and abiding commitment to helping each other Never forget the worst of where you came from and that others may be in similar circumstances Stress the need to champion equity in ladders of opportunity not guaranteed equal outcomes	Should conduct evaluations collaboratively Must deliver on commitments Should conduct evaluations to help assure that programs will effectively improve the lives of intended beneficiaries Insisted on training new evaluators by having them work from the lowest to highest levels Assure evaluations are equitable in addressing the needs of the full range of a program's stakeholders, especially the poor and disadvantaged Beware of the trap of developing a dependent class by creating a culture of government welfare
He grew up in a small Iowa town and appreciated the blessing of living in the United States and associated values.	Learned through experience the value of neighbors helping neighbors Appreciation for citizenship in a free society and learning early the precepts of democracy, the rule of law, and conviction that every person should be able to advance as far and as high as their God-given talents and hard work will take them	Stakeholder engagement … needed & useful for getting sound evaluations done and applied Strong orientation in the Joint Committee standards to the U.S. Constitution, including especially its Bill of Rights Employment of an evaluator career ladder in developing evaluators and evaluation-oriented leaders
Substituting in 40+ inner-city Chicago schools opened his eyes to problems/values.	"… I concluded I might be the only person [in Chicago] who knew how bad things were across the district, especially in the inner city schools."	[This experience] influenced me [years later] to include context evaluation—assessments of needs, problems, assets, and opportunities—into my CIPP Model evaluation approach.

appeared to be their opposites in his personal life. He offered rational critiques for evaluating wartime valor, his mother's decisions, parapsychological phenomena, product evaluation, critical-thinking education, and eventually colleagues' ideas about professional evaluation. Those professional evaluation critiques became his main contributions to the field, which have had enduring and extensive influence on professional evaluators.

NEW DIRECTIONS FOR EVALUATION • DOI: 10.1002/ev

Table 9.5. Eleanor Chelimsky's connections

Areas of connection	Examples of connections	Manifestation in professional evaluations and views
Parents influenced her values, especially employing rationality in methods and defending evaluations made.	"My parents ... were big on rational decision making, and I was taught early on to try to envisage all potential costs and benefits when making choices ... although my parents were good about letting me make at least some decisions for myself, I always had to explain exactly how I came to make them."	"So as I look at it from a 'connections' point of view, my parents gave me a two-edged gift there—not only the habit of thinking about potential losses and longer-term gains, but also the confidence necessary to make decisions—which has certainly been useful to me ... in evaluation."
Piano performance experiences taught important evaluation methods and values that apply to other evaluation situations.	"One thing that is basic to performing classical music, in addition to the normal analytical work involved in music study and learning, is the need for synthetic thinking. A musician must gracefully combine form and content ... But the style of the music ... must also be integrated into that form and content, and the whole performance and program carefully considered from the viewpoint of its likely audience."	" ... this is not so different from evaluation. We have the same job of analysis in reaching an evaluative conclusion, and also the same requirement for synthesis, when integrating context, questions, methods, data, practitioner/participant experience, and user needs, as we try to say what happened in a program, how well it worked, or how our findings should be used ... As a result, perhaps because musical training had driven me in this direction ... I was always looking for the more perfect synthesis, constantly adding to the kinds of things that needed to be considered in an evaluation design ... "
Living in post-World War II Paris, France, clarified values to take into account.	"I lived in France for nearly 20 years (1948–1967), and there are two specific lessons I learned there that ... deeply affected my approach to evaluation. The first was the discovery that a strong networking effort [Sartre and the French political left] could have amazing effects on shaping public opinion and policy making; the second was that, no matter how excellent and exhaustive that networking effort ... a single credible voice (Solzhenitsyn) could demolish its achievements in the blink of an eye."	"I carried away two ideas from these events that I later used in my evaluation work: (a) the value of networking as a means to credibility, and (b) the power of a credible dissenting voice to disrupt that networking."

Table 9.6. Ernie House's connections

Areas of connection	Examples of connections	Manifestation in professional evaluations and views
Teachers' and stepfather's influence bolstered rejection of some values and acceptance of others.	"From these and other experiences, I developed a strong resolve and motivation not to be controlled by others."	"Years later these traits became useful in evaluation. Often I can see what others do not see, and I will say what others will not say."
Influence of mother, uncles, and other adults solidified these same values but from different angles.	"Another conclusion I had reached by the age of eight was that adults made bad decisions that could prove disastrous for them and for my sister and me … At an early age I began looking beneath the surface of people and events, and I looked suspiciously. This attitude evolved into an intellectual style."	"All people practice willful ignorance to a greater or lesser degree. They choose not to see things—a luxury I felt I could not afford. I pushed willful ignorance back further than most people can tolerate. In books, articles, and high-profile evaluations, I employed these skills."
Investing in the stock market helped him articulate evaluation methods and attitudes.	"… when I began managing my retirement funds, I found investing fascinating. In a way it was a pure form of evaluation that culminated in concrete gains and losses, unlike contemplating the inadequacy of Hume's theory of causation. And I was good at it."	"Investing requires skills—skills of skepticism similar to those I had developed in evaluation."

Stufflebeam adopted the values of his parents and small Iowa community into his evaluations of himself as a student and later into evaluating students and others when he became a teacher and coach. He valued maintaining a strong work ethic, championing equity and fairness, helping neighbors develop self-reliance, and appreciating citizenship in a free society; and he was willing to give up position and status when his values were being threatened. As his career led him into professional evaluation, he integrated these values into his CIPP approach, his collaborative orientation, his reasons for doing evaluation, his mentoring of others who wanted to become professional evaluators, and his career-long efforts to create and promote meta-evaluation standards.

Chelimsky developed confidence in using many of her values from her parents' examples and their challenges to her to rationally defend her childhood evaluations and decisions. She built on that confidence to expand her

Table 9.7. Michael Quinn Patton's connections

Areas of connection	Examples of connections	Manifestation in professional evaluations and views
Religious and paternal values encouraged him to choose his own values and live with the consequences.	"The church minister and youth religious leaders didn't give us rules. They ... told us to study the Bible and decide ..." My father also took that perspective. He had strong opinions, but he always emphasized personal choice and looking at the implications of those choices. In that message, there was a lot of personal responsibility, a sense of implications that come from actions, and you have to decide what the choices are.	"... every action has consequences, so examine the potential consequences." Keep your options open. "Look at how things are unfolding as they unfold. If what you're doing isn't working, change what you're doing."
Experience of being a youth revivalist speaker taught him to speak and analyze in evaluation situations.	"I came to understand, as I was working to enhance my performance, that ... People were responding to being challenged on whether they were living their lives in accordance with the teachings of Jesus." I learned to be quite an effective speaker as a result of those opportunities, and lots and lots of practice.	My public speaking skills and my analytical skills both come out of those experiences, of parsing Bible verses, of speaking and getting feedback, and of figuring out what people responded to.
Conversion to humanism and to the practice of seeing life from many different perspectives led to the values he built into his approach to evaluation.	I made it an evaluation exercise, inviting people to evaluate their lives against these criteria and decide whether or not they matched up. My religious transformation ended up bringing me to a place of having to examine in life what's working and not working according to these principles.	"An ongoing emphasis in my evaluation practice carries forward from those Baptist revival experiences of inviting people to look at what they believe, look at what they're doing, look at the disparate nature of what they're doing compared to what they believe, and do reality testing about whether they're doing the things they believe and whether they're accomplishing the things that they want to accomplish. That reality testing theme intersects with my interest in multiple perspectives, both of which derive from the early life experiences I've described here."

NEW DIRECTIONS FOR EVALUATION • DOI: 10.1002/ev

values and apply them in evaluation as a concert pianist and as a critical observer of French intellectuals and society. Perhaps subconsciously she applied this array of values and valuing to her professional evaluation assignments in highly publicized projects and organizations—many of them before she thought of herself as a professional evaluator.

House learned skepticism early from the adults he observed: a father who died early, a mother who did her best under trying circumstances, a stepfather who was psychotic, uncles who were in trouble with the law, and teachers who used behavioristic rewards to try to motivate him. Thus, he learned to question authority, to look below the surface, to be willing to see what others don't and say what others won't, and to be suspicious of others' claims. He used these values to guide his performance of high-profile evaluations when he was thrust into them and used the associated lessons to write about evaluation, enabling the profession to learn from his experiences.

Patton learned from his parents and religious leaders to evaluate possible consequences of his options and then live with the consequences of his own evaluations and decisions. He developed a pragmatist value perspective that he lived by in his youthful evangelistic experiences, educational choices, marriages, and child-rearing practices, which he aptly expressed in one of his evaluation principles: "If what you're doing isn't working, change what you're doing." He used these values when obligation required him to preach after he had lost his own faith in his religion, allowing values to guide his public speaking, Biblical analysis, and invitations to others to evaluate their own lives and criteria for judging themselves. He continued using these values as he became a professional evaluator and educator—creating, writing about, and applying utilization-focused, developmental, and principles-based evaluation approaches. Reality testing is the main value that runs through his evaluation life experiences, extraprofessional and professional.

Subthemes

As we look across these cases, subthemes emerge regarding the use of values from these individuals' extraprofessional lives in conceptualizing and conducting their professional evaluations.

First, each evaluator is unique, as is each reader of these cases. Though they share many common values (see below), these seven grew as individuals into their own particular value sets, comprised both common and unique principles and standards, which they use to evaluate a wide variety of evaluands in their personal lives. Many of these values are manifest also in their professional views, which influence the field in individual ways, as people with similar values want to consider these evaluators and/or their ideas in their own evaluations.

Second, as demonstrated by their descriptions of their evaluation lives, these evaluators share some common patterns, values, and/or beliefs:

- Their professional evaluation approaches exemplify how they have formalized learning experiences from their extraprofessional evaluations to use in conducting formal evaluations.
- People and programs can improve, and evaluation supports improvement in life generally as well as in professional contexts.
- Society needs better evaluation. Finding ways to improve extraprofessional *and* professional evaluation warrants our attention.
- In all cases, rationality and reason are highly valued as central to good evaluation. But professional evaluations may require flexibility in defining rationality. They may draw on many ways of knowing, thinking, judging, deciding, choosing, and evaluating, which often include considering intuition and emotion, relying on feelings of confidence and peace, and trusting gut reactions.
- All participants evaluate continuously as part of living, and they constantly translate their values into criteria for deciding what they and others should accomplish.
- All participants have been influenced in their value choices by their culture, parents and other adults, peers, formal educational experiences, religious values or a shift away from the religion of their youth, political views and leaders, and views of their own personality. But they have a lot of choice in how they respond to these influences.

Questions Raised

In addition to these themes, study of the cases has raised several questions that could be used to continue this inquiry with other cases and to hypothesize (and test with later studies) how professional evaluators connect their professional and extraprofessional evaluation lives:

- Do different ways of identifying quality provide important windows for understanding how evaluators think about and conduct their evaluations?
- Do interpretive frameworks from various disciplines in which evaluators are educated provide important bases for their professional evaluation thinking?
- How do evaluators' relationships with stakeholders in and outside professional evaluations emphasize and expand characteristics of their studies?
- How does culture influence professional evaluators' values and evaluation lives?
- How does making extraprofessional evaluations and dealing with their consequences help evaluators learn what they value most and how to use

those values in making both extraprofessional and professional evaluations?

- How might intuition, rational thought, individual personality, or a blend of influences such as genetics, parenting, and culture invite people to be attracted to some values more than others?
- How do people use various combinations of rationality and intuition in making evaluations and learn to discern which evaluation choices and values they want to pursue in the future and which to avoid?
- How do people use evaluation to enhance their learning experiences, including how to know if a formal evaluation is warranted, what approach options are available, how to improve their evaluations, and how to improve their evaluation abilities? Does this information strengthen the view of evaluation as a *transdiscipline*? What implications does it suggest for evaluation education and capacity building?

Comments by Each Author About the Other Authors' Articles

Comments by Robert Stake

I did not need to read David Williams' collection to know that professional evaluators have little in common. Experience has taught me that we are as diverse as the population of people who do not evaluate professionally. When charged formally with responsibility to evaluate, among ourselves we define the task differently, we choose different criteria, and we work toward different uses to which the findings may be put. We do not have the causal diagnostics which constrain the pharmacologist and architect.

Formative and summative doesn't tell of the diversity, nor does quantitative and qualitative. Nor will Michael Scriven's life search for limits constrain evaluators to biographical chapters, were they submitted to David from all the others in the world. I think the universes of these humanities are born of expansion and defy the concept of limits.

Even when the methods are prescribed and purposes and contexts established, we evaluation colleagues do not agree. We disagree as to which training regimen is most fitting and as to who would be the best committee chairperson. We sometimes yearn for more common ground—and CIPP was a good place to start—but is our diversity and resistance to standardization not a blessing?

The stories of these seven evaluators are probably as similar and dissimilar as those of any seven others. Each deserves a following, but collectively no rubric. The experience and insight and age and connection to education of these good people do not provide grounds for knowing from whence standards should come nor the dispositions to which evaluation should be put. And are we not blessed that we are not more homogeneous than we are?

There are few program evaluation situations in which quality can in consensus be defined. It often will be useful to try to agree on criteria and critical incidents. It often will be useful to postulate purposes of the evaluand and methods of communicating with stakeholders. But we evaluators are as much driven to invention and uniqueness in our approaches and metaphors as by any need to have common valuing.

In their articles, Eleanor Chelimsky, Michael Patton, and Marv Alkin trace their inclination to serve the audience. It is an ethic of importance to us all. Unfortunately, we are seldom wise enough to know how to serve them best. And we have another ethic: to speak truth to power, to convey perception and assertion that are not welcome. Where to strike the compromise between service and confrontation? It will differ from evaluator to evaluator. What good is served to make the striking impersonal?

The human condition is served little by precise handling of gross approximates. And all the measures of effort and accomplishment, cost and benefit, sacrifice and valor are but simple placeholders for human valuing. We work to improve our approximates, but should not fail to say that others could have been better. We serve our audiences by insisting on the conditionality that Ernie House was long ago advised against.

What is the merit of diversity? It is no different for a profession than for a people. The merit is in stretching the limits of experience and understanding. It helps to have great men and women proclaiming understanding and explanation, and the individuals assessing both should be noticed, but the greatest knowing is the knowing that the people hold together. It will arise from different experience, and voice different values, but their knowledge collectively will be greater than the best of lone voices. We are blessed in having such diversity in our profession.

Comments by Marvin Alkin

David Williams has commented on a common theme that he believes pervades each of the papers. That common theme of values and valuing is certainly evident in the papers as I read them. Beyond that, it is difficult to see a large number of commonalities across the papers. This may be because the writing style and perspective of the authors are so very different. It may also be because of my personal inability to dig deep enough to discern additional commonalities.

I do see a number of minor themes that exist in many but not all of the papers. First, there is a concern about wanting to make a difference. For some, the nature of making a difference is captured on a grander social scale. For others, it is more incremental—thinking about one program at a time. Although there are subthemes of this orientation, this theme persists.

Some view this theme with a strong attention to maximizing the possibility that evaluation use occurs, believing that through use programs will improve. Others focus on the political context and the obstacles that evaluation faces. Still others emphasize the broader goal of improving the world through the evaluative pursuit of seeking social justice. The authors, respectively, are Patton, Chelimsky, and House.

I see another theme of attention to communication, focusing again on the same three authors. We have seen Patton commenting on how he learned to understand an audience and tailor messages to sway that audience. Chelimsky has noted the need to recognize and tailor reports at GAO to a variety of political constituencies. And House has recognized argumentation as a part of the evaluator's repertoire in order to communicate.

Other authors may also have contributed to these themes, but their views were not as strongly discernable. The themes are certainly present in my own article as well.

Comments by Michael Scriven

The first instinct of an inquiring mind looking at these autobiothoughts is to search for something in common that pointed us toward evaluation. There are a few cases where at least some childhood experience showed we'd started on that path very early, but that just raises the question of why we started on that track as children, to which I don't see any answer except genes. It has occurred to me that what may be a more important search—in terms of lessons learnt for future implementation (e.g., in raising our children or students)—is for experiences or influences that led to another essential property that, it seems to me, most of us share to an unusual extent.

That property is risk-tolerance. When we started looking at evaluation as a thing to study, not just a thing to do, it was pretty close to the peak of the value-free takeover in the social sciences, which not only meant you could not get a job teaching about evaluation, since it was a non-subject scientifically speaking, but you could not get your thoughts published in social science journals since there was an editorial ban on the topic. (Thank goodness for the educational journals!) That meant that people like Stufflebeam, Stake, and their colleagues, who simply went ahead anyway, were risking their careers and reputations. It was easier for people like me, because my day job was in philosophy and, theoretically at least, more or less anything is a legitimate topic in philosophy. (But actually within my subspecialty, which was philosophy of science, it was frowned on fairly seriously for decades after the Evaluation Network began.)

In any case, there are some clues in the bios about hard times in our youth that suggest we share a certain grittiness that made survival possible. My take from that is to make sure that in the capacity building that we hope will lead to new thought leaders, we stress some affective characteristics as well as the cognitive repertoire required. Not that it's as necessary today as then—but the thought may be just a sign one is slipping into the rut of a new paradigm.

This ties in with the view that one sometimes hears from Nobelers, that the "new paradigm" players get short shrift in the competition for funding and recognition in their early days, probably because the reviewers are mostly "existing paradigm" loyalists. This is easily understandable, but less than ideal, and there are a number of ways of counterbalancing this loading against radical reconsideration: for example, an innovation "set-aside" of 5 or 10 percent of the available funding for "outside the box" proposals or small funding organizations focused almost exclusively on such proposals, like Faster Forward Foundation, which has just opened for business.

The above thoughts are not just reflections on the past, but part of what we should recognize as a relatively new branch of evaluation that I'm calling "meta-disciplinary evaluation:" the critical evaluation of whole or part of disciplines. Work by Chris Coryn on the actual quality of peer review and by John Ioannidis on the actual truth of replicability has shown that serious investigation rather than pious incantation reveals a pair of pathetically incompetent practices, much in need of reform by applying common standards of objectivity and validity from evaluation practice.

Comments by Daniel Stufflebeam

When I agreed to participate in this project, I expected that in the end—after having read the life experience accounts of the other six "early evaluators"—I would be able to extract some pervasive, profound, or nearly profound themes about the seven evaluators' values that would be of interest and use to students and practitioners of evaluation and clients of evaluators. With a major exception—the importance of learning evaluation by doing evaluation—I have not identified especially noteworthy themes that cut across all seven evaluation stories and can't add much to Dr. Williams' summary of the seven accounts. However, the accounts do provide interesting background about each author's developmental years, trials faced, and experiences that shaped his or her evaluation insights and contributions. Through these accounts many readers will gain a better understanding of each evaluation theorist per se.

A few points that I jotted down as I read the accounts follow:

1. Life experiences can substantially help shape one's concept of evaluation. This was clear in a couple of the accounts but not so much in the others. Especially poignant were Eleanor Chelimsky's references to music as a metaphor for thinking about evaluation and to her time in Europe where she gained a special appreciation for the power of networking and of never giving up in a quest to bring about social justice. Also Michael Scriven stressed the importance of his early interest in and sustained employment of the study of critical thinking as a foundation for serious work in evaluation.

2. Through leading complex evaluation efforts, one can develop procedures and mechanisms that (I think) many organizations could employ to set up and operate effective evaluation systems that can institutionalize and mainstream sound evaluation. Chelimsky's piece is especially pertinent here, concerning how at GAO she employed an

evaluation credibility checklist, role playing for preparing to deliver effective evaluation reports, "murder boards" for "after action" reviews of evaluations, advisory boards, and visiting scholars.

3. Networking with colleagues is a powerful means of developing one's concept and approach to evaluation. This is seen especially in Stake's interactions with evaluators in England's East Anglia school of evaluation and his exchanges with such American scholars as Cronbach, Scriven, Hastings, and House.

4. Education plays an important role in equipping one to conduct sound evaluations and contribute to the development of evaluation theory and practice, but relevant educational experiences for different evaluators may vary widely and extend far beyond courses in program evaluation. I found it interesting that none of the seven "early evaluators," myself included, had been trained in evaluation. Each one built on instruction received in such diverse areas as philosophy, critical thinking, piano and music composition, measurement and statistics, sociology, counseling and guidance, clinical psychology, mathematics, biblical training, and administration. Dr. Williams illustrates the more recent breed of evaluators who have been trained specifically in evaluation theory and methods.

Overall, the seven accounts do underscore the power of learning evaluation by doing evaluation.

Comments by Eleanor Chelimsky

As I see it, the importance of this project is that if we as evaluators can learn to know and understand our own value biases and correct for them, we will have narrowed in some small way that area of uncertainty that exists for all scientific and evaluative endeavors, regardless of methodology (Campbell, 1984; Dyson, 2012). So I think the basic questions the project will need to answer are (a) Can searching one's memory call up the relevant events and nonevents that characterize pre-evaluation values/experiences and relate them persuasively to particular stances in evaluation? and (b) How good is memory as a tool for such an inquiry?

Reading through my co-authors' contributions to this effort, it seems as if my answer to the first question is probably yes. We can, for example, trace the training we've received, the life crises we've endured, and the particular balances we've had to make—between the confusions of reality and the seductions of pure form, between rebellions against rationality and its acceptance or compromise, between tidy quantitative representations of people's worlds and their actual lived experience. And we have few problems identifying their effects on our work.

But the second question may be another matter. Given the kind of good faith and honesty we see in this project, we can, I think, be sure of the quality of the recollections (and the validity of their connections to evaluation), but not, perhaps, their quantity. Yet this is obviously important because contrary suppressed memories can threaten the validity of an entire value structure. In evaluation we've learned a lot about problems of recall, and they are not so different from those Augustine described in his examination of the layers of memory, circa 397 AD:

> I arrive in the fields and vast mansions of memory, where are treasured innumerable images brought in there from objects of every conceivable kind perceived by the senses. There too are hidden away the modified images we produce when by our thinking we magnify or diminish or in any way alter the information our senses have reported. There too is everything else that has been consigned and stowed away, and not yet engulfed and buried in oblivion. Sojourning there I command something I want to present itself, and immediately certain things emerge, while others have to be pursued for some time and dug out from remote crannies. Others again come tumbling out in disorderly profusion, and leap into prominence as though asking, "Are we what you want?" when it is something different that I am asking for and trying to recall. (Augustine, 1997, pp. 244–245)

So in pursuing this effort my sense is that—as always in evaluation—we have to remember that there may be major unknowns lurking in those "vast mansions of memory." We should, of course, try to improve the process of examining our past, but we can certainly take heart in any ability we achieve that can reduce even partially those obstinate areas of enduring evaluative uncertainty.

Comments by Ernie House

How did my colleagues and I develop the independent critical reasoning at the heart of evaluation? At an early age both Scriven and I lost fathers and were cared for by mothers who were in difficult circumstances. We both determined that we would have to assess and negotiate the world by our own reasoning. Before long Scriven was probing the basis of religion, science, and eventually evaluation. By high school I was reading Freud and diagnosing my mother's illnesses, a service she did not appreciate. Later, I examined concepts like values, validity, and justice in evaluation. Alkin watched, questioned, and argued with his grocer father, whose kind nature was taken advantage of by customers. Alkin made rational decision making a focus of his career, extending the idea into evaluation. He could help improve the decisions of others, if not those of his father.

Chelimsky and Patton became accomplished performers. As performers and evaluators, they spent considerable time studying their audiences. Chelimsky practiced music and rehearsed her reasoning about key decisions before her attentive parents. Recalling her Paris years, she worked in evaluation to reduce "group think," a severe Washington social disease. Patton, as youthful evangelist, perfected his persuasive delivery, measured by the amount garnered in congregational contributions. After abandoning religion, he used his formidable speaking skills to promote humanitarian goals in evaluation, often with dramatic flair.

Stake absorbed two opposing orientations, one from his pharmacist father, dedicated to producing quality products, and one from his compassionate teacher mother, concerned about people. The interplay between these views produced an enigmatic perspective. Sometimes he swings from one to the other, surprising associates by shifting from measurement to case study or from caring mentor to taskmaster. He takes positions intuitively and looks for reasons to support them.

Stufflebeam fully accepted the ideals of his family, church, and community. He ascribes his core values of hard work, resilience, and reliability to the rigors of growing up in a small Iowa town. He applied these virtues to new situations, as in the ghetto schools of Chicago and the field of evaluation. In developing evaluation standards, he worked diligently to instill virtue in his colleagues.

Comments by Michael Patton

These stories brought to mind Malcolm Gladwell's book on *Outliers* (2007), which examined what distinguishes high achievers like Mozart and Bill Gates. Along with talent, intelligence, and ambition, Gladwell found that high-performing outliers benefited from some fortunate opportunity to intensively cultivate a skill that became the bedrock of their contributions and achievements. However, as prominent as any other explanatory factor, Gladwell concluded—indeed, more prominent and decisive than other factors—was luck.

In a similar vein, Jim Collins and Mort Hansen (2011) studied factors explaining the success of those few multinational companies (outliers) that flourished in the aftermath of the 2008 global financial meltdown. In the face of uncertainty and chaos, luck played a big part, as did the capacity to recognize and take advantage of lucky opportunity and good fortune.

Concomitant with my reviewing the intriguing and provocative stories of these colleagues, a report was published (2015) in the journal *Science* by Cristian Tomasetti and Bert Vogelstein, cancer scientists at Johns Hopkins University School of Medicine, concluding that the risk of developing many kinds of cancer is a matter of random luck. More specifically, though cancers are known to result from life styles, inherited proclivities, and environmental exposures, many cancers result from random mutations that happen when healthy stem cells divide.

You can see where this is going. There is good fortune and bad. As I received these stories from David Williams, a colleague and friend,

Brenda Zimmerman, was killed in a car accident in Toronto. Brenda was coauthor with me of *Getting to Maybe: How the World Is Changed* (Westley, Zimmerman, & Patton, 2006), which found that successful social movements emerged through taking advantage of fortuitous opportunities in complex circumstances. She was my mentor in complexity theory, which frames my *Developmental Evaluation* book (Patton, 2011); Chapter 4 in that book opens by describing her influence on my work and on the field more generally. She died 12 years younger than I am.

So although the stories in this issue focus on our childhoods, I come away from reading them mindful of our fortuitous longevity. Several of these colleagues have faced and are facing major health challenges. Carol Weiss is no longer with us. But in the end we are all included in this issue because we have had the good fortune, the luck, to live long and have the support of colleagues, friends, and families. Chance and opportunity may well be the major explanatory factors. But as Pasteur famously asserted: "Chance favors the prepared mind."

Implications for the Future of Evaluation (David Williams)

Readers may be seeking ways to apply this book's content personally. I have learned from this study that understanding my own life journey in evaluation from childhood to present and projecting that life into the future helps me clarify the values as well as evaluation activities I engage in professionally and otherwise. I realize from studying the lived experiences of others that how I understand evaluation, how I practice it, and who I am becoming as an evaluator are much more central to how I treat other stakeholders, audiences, coparticipants (basically all other people), and how I serve them than any of the methods I've learned and use. I agree with a professional musician and choir director/professor who said about his evaluation life, "I'm still learning to listen for quality, and always will be, because my understanding of quality is continually growing."

So, I invite you as readers to examine your values: how you have learned them, whether you are still learning about them, and how you may use them to strengthen evaluation in your extraprofessional as well as your professional evaluation life. Exploring the following issues and questions may help:

Issues

• When acting as a professional evaluator or hiring one, we're not limited to being methodologists. We're acting as unique persons with a rich set of values we have accumulated over our lifetime and through our culture. How we apply those values may fit well with stakeholders' values or conflict with them. Each case involves tailoring to fit the value combinations of unique individuals.

- When we try to follow an approach of an evaluation theorist, we ought to explore the values that are implied by that individual's approach and decide if they are compatible with our values and with the values of our stakeholders and participants.
- When we share our evaluation plans, activities, findings, and recommendations with stakeholders, they are evaluating us and our offerings from their value perspectives, even if they are unaware of doing this. Being open about this unspoken evaluation may be helpful.
- We should ask how well we are taking our values and our stakeholders' values into account in our work or if we are somehow assuming the value-free research perspective criticized by Scriven (1991).
- Our evaluation culture may be shifting as our values shift over time. We should meta-evaluate that shift along the way to decide if our evaluations are becoming stronger or weaker with our shifting values.
- Because different stakeholders have different values and views on values, we as evaluators need to clarify which values should be given power and respect when value conflicts surface.
- All who are involved in evaluation should think carefully about how they and their values are influencing the field generally and their own stakeholders in particular. We all grow up learning certain values from adults and peers, including methodological inequities. We adjust these values over years of experiencing extraprofessional evaluations we do and observe. And like the people represented in this issue, we may find that these experiences are relevant to our professional evaluations and theories in a variety of ways.

Questions

- How do you interpret the stories told throughout this issue?
- How do you critique the authors' interpretations?
- How might you apply the experiences of the evaluators reported here to your own evaluation practices and theorizing?
- How well do you understand your own and your stakeholders' evaluation life experiences and values and what difference might that make in your work? If you don't understand them well, how could you find out more about them?
- How might your own extraprofessional evaluation life experiences be shaping your approaches to professional evaluation practice and/or theorizing?
- How might you use better understanding of your stakeholders' extraprofessional evaluation experiences and expectations to tailor professional evaluations that address those experiences and expectations?
- What implications do you find in this study for involving stakeholders as participants in professional evaluations?

- What implications do you find in this study for enhancing professional evaluation use?

Moving Forward

If you would like to get involved in this project, please e-mail ddwbyu@gmail.com about participating in the study. But also consider interacting with your collaborating evaluation teams and stakeholders/clients/audiences in ways that will encourage this kind of reflection often and continually. Then share what you learn with your students and with the rest of us so we can all learn ways to improve our evaluation skills and abilities.

References

Alkin, M. C., Vo, A. T., & Christie, C. A. (2012). The evaluator's role in valuing: Who and with whom. In G. Julnes (Ed.), *Promoting valuation in the public interest: Informing policies for judging value in evaluation. New Directions for Evaluation, 133*, 29–41.

Augustine (circa 398 AD/ trans. 1997). *The confessions* (M. Boulding, Trans.; J. E. Rotelle, Ed.). Hyde Park, NY: New City Press.

Campbell, D. (1984). Numbers and narrative. In R. Light & D. Pillemer (Eds.), *Summing up: The science of reviewing research* (pp. 104–143). Cambridge, MA: Harvard University Press.

Chelimsky, E. (2012). Valuing, evaluation methods, and the politicization of the evaluation process. *New Directions for Evaluation, 133*, 77–83.

Collins, J., & Hansen, M. (2011). *Great by choice: Uncertainty, chaos, and luck—Why some thrive despite them all.* New York, NY: HarperBusiness.

Dyson, F. (2012, April 5). Science on the rampage. *The New York Review of Books.* Retrieved from http://www.nybooks.com/articles/archives/2012/apr/05/science-rampage-natural-philosophy/.

Gladwell, M. (2007). *Outliers: The story of success.* Boston, MA: Little, Brown and Company.

Hart, J. G., & Embree, L. (Eds.). (1997) *Phenomenology of values and valuing.* In N. de Warren & D. Moran (Series Eds.), *Contributions to phenomenology* (Vol. 28). New York, NY: Kluwer Academic.

House, E. R., & Howe, K. R. (1999). *Values in evaluation and social research.* Thousand Oaks, CA: Sage.

Patton, M. Q. (2008). *Utilization-focused evaluation* (4th ed.). Thousand Oaks, CA: Sage.

Patton, M. Q. (2011) *Developmental evaluation.* New York, NY: Guilford.

Scriven, M. (1991). *Evaluation thesaurus* (4th ed.). Newbury Park, CA: Sage.

Scriven, M. (2013). *Key evaluation checklist.* Retrieved from http://www.michaelscriven.info/images/KEC_3.22.2013.pdf.

Stake, R.E. (2004). *Standards-based and responsive evaluation.* Thousand Oaks, CA: Sage.

Stufflebeam, D. L. (2001). Evaluation models. *New Directions for Evaluation, 89*, 7–98.

Tomasetti, C., & Vogelstein, B. (2015). Variation in cancer risk among tissues can be explained by the number of stem cell divisions. *Science 347*(6217), 78–81.

Westley, F., Zimmerman, B., & Patton, M.Q. (2006) *Getting to maybe: How the world is changed.* Toronto, Canada: Random House Canada

DAVID D. WILLIAMS is a professor of Instructional Psychology and Technology at Brigham Young University.

INDEX

ORDER FORM SUBSCRIPTION AND SINGLE ISSUES

DISCOUNTED BACK ISSUES:

Use this form to receive 20% off all back issues of *New Directions for Evaluation*.
All single issues priced at **$23.20** (normally $29.00)

TITLE	ISSUE NO.	ISBN
_____	_____	_____
_____	_____	_____
_____	_____	_____

Call 1-800-835-6770 or see mailing instructions below. When calling, mention the promotional code JBNND to receive your discount. For a complete list of issues, please visit www.wiley.com/WileyCDA/WileyTitle/productCd-EV.html

SUBSCRIPTIONS: (1 YEAR, 4 ISSUES)

☐ New Order   ☐ Renewal

U.S.	☐ Individual: $89	☐ Institutional: $380
CANADA/MEXICO	☐ Individual: $89	☐ Institutional: $422
ALL OTHERS	☐ Individual: $113	☐ Institutional: $458

Call 1-800-835-6770 or see mailing and pricing instructions below.
Online subscriptions are available at www.onlinelibrary.wiley.com

ORDER TOTALS:

Issue / Subscription Amount: $ _____

Shipping Amount: $ _____
(for single issues only – subscription prices include shipping)

Total Amount: $ _____

SHIPPING CHARGES:
First Item $6.00
Each Add'l Item $2.00

(No sales tax for U.S. subscriptions. Canadian residents, add GST for subscription orders. Individual rate subscriptions must be paid by personal check or credit card. Individual rate subscriptions may not be resold as library copies.)

BILLING & SHIPPING INFORMATION:

☐ **PAYMENT ENCLOSED:** *(U.S. check or money order only. All payments must be in U.S. dollars.)*

☐ **CREDIT CARD:**   ☐ VISA   ☐ MC   ☐ AMEX

Card number _____Exp. Date_____

Card Holder Name_____Card Issue # _____

Signature _____Day Phone_____

☐ **BILL ME:** *(U.S. institutional orders only. Purchase order required.)*

Purchase order # _____
Federal Tax ID 13559302 • GST 89102-8052

Name_____

Address_____

Phone_____ E-mail_____

Copy or detach page and send to: **John Wiley & Sons, Inc. / Jossey Bass**
PO Box 55381
Boston, MA 02205-9850

PROMO JBNND